A ℛABBI
LOOKS AT THE
SUPERNATURAL

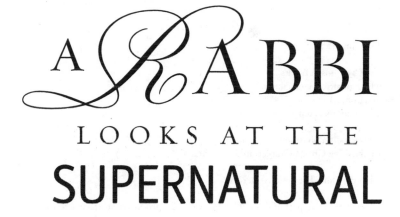

A RABBI

LOOKS AT THE

SUPERNATURAL

*A Revealing Look at Angels, Demons,
Miracles, Heaven and Hell*

JONATHAN BERNIS

Chosen

a division of Baker Publishing Group
Minneapolis, Minnesota

© 2016 by Jonathan Bernis

Published by Chosen Books
11400 Hampshire Avenue South
Bloomington, Minnesota 55438
www.chosenbooks.com

Chosen Books is a division of
Baker Publishing Group, Grand Rapids, Michigan

Printed in the United States of America

Library of Congress Control Number: 2016942347

ISBN 978-0-8007-9786-7 (trade paper)
ISBN 978-0-8007-9821-5 (cloth)

Cover design by Rob Williams, InsideOutCreativeArts

16 17 18 19 20 21 22   7 6 5 4 3 2 1

This book is dedicated to my beloved mother,
who is not yet a believer in Yeshua.
May you discover the supernatural power
of the living God in the twilight of your life.

I have been praying for you for more than
35 years. Lord, please answer my prayer.

Contents

Acknowledgments

I would like to thank Dave Wimbish, my faithful and talented writer and researcher for more than a decade. Dave, you are amazing!

I also want to acknowledge Catherine Cooker for her excellent work on the manuscript. Catherine, you are one of the most thorough and professional editors I have ever worked with.

To Jane Campbell and the excellent team at Chosen: This is the fourth book I have done with you, and I am still happy as a clam working with you. Well, maybe not a clam since I try to keep kosher . . . but, seriously, you all have been great to work with.

Finally, I want to thank my dedicated and hard-working team at Jewish Voice. It is a joy and honor to work with people so committed to saving and transforming lives—"to the Jew first and also to the Nations."

Dust in the Wind?

Why is there something, anything, rather than nothing? In our fascination with life's origin and evolution, we bypass this most basic of conundrums. The very fact and nature of existence . . . force upon us the unsettling reality that at some level there is the metaphysical.

Gerald L. Schroeder[1]

Why are we here?
Are we simply a random collection of atoms that have come together for a brief time—atoms that will soon disappear like a puff of smoke, leaving nothing at all behind? Are we, as the seventies rock band Kansas declared, merely "dust in the wind"? Sound and fury signifying nothing?

Or is there more to our existence? A purpose and a plan behind our very brief appearance in history?

And how about this—is there more to this world than we can comprehend with our physical senses? Is anything out there beyond what we can see, hear, taste, touch and smell?

In other words, is there a supernatural realm of angels, demons, seers, prophets, spirits and the like? Or is the "supernatural" merely an invention of charlatans like palm readers and spirit mediums to take advantage of the gullible?

People have been asking such questions since the first people stared in amazement and awe at the brilliance of the nighttime sky. They have been debated by philosophers, scientists, members of the clergy, educators and ordinary people from all walks of life. Some have invested years of wisdom, energy and hard work into "proving" that life is merely a matter of chance. Others have worked just as hard and long "proving" the existence of what might be called a divine purpose.

Obviously, these are not questions that I will resolve to everyone's satisfaction in the few pages of this book. But I will come as close as I can. My intention is to investigate the matter as thoroughly and fairly as possible and present my honest conclusions—conclusions based on more than three decades of study and experience as a Messianic rabbi.

We will start off with a close-up look at the universe we live in. Can it be explained as a random act of nature, or is something more behind it all? Is the Bible true when it says, "In the beginning, God created the heavens and the earth"? Or is that merely a parable to explain scientific concepts that ancient human beings could never hope to comprehend?

Once we have taken a look at the physical universe, we will move on to the invisible, spiritual side of creation. We will talk about the existence of God and the problem of evil—if a good God exists, why does He allow bad things to happen to good people? We will also discuss topics like these:

- The nature and reality of sin
- Miracles
- The existence of heaven and hell
- The meaning of life

As you can see, it will get pretty deep before we are through.

About the Author

Now, you may be wondering what it means when I call myself a "Messianic rabbi." It means, first of all, that I believe that Jesus (I like to call Him by His Hebrew given name, Yeshua) is the Messiah. I also believe, like the early followers of Yeshua, that I am still very much Jewish.

Most Jews of my generation will not refer to me as a rabbi, because *rabbi*, in the Jewish world, means someone who has studied at a recognized Jewish institution and has been ordained by a mainstream, recognized Jewish body. Though I do not meet these criteria, I am ordained and have served in full-time ministry for more than thirty years.

One other very important thing that qualifies me to write this book is that I am a naturally curious person. I am not content with pat answers to tough questions. I want to find the right answers for myself, and I am willing to work hard to find them. If I do not know enough about a subject to answer it on my own, I find experts who know the subject well and see what they have to say about it.

Not long ago at a dinner, I found myself seated next to a distinguished-looking, well-spoken gentleman. I could tell that he had a good grasp on current events and seemed to know what was going on in the world.

During the course of our conversation, he asked if I knew that the pyramids were built by ancient aliens. I have no idea how he steered the conversation to that subject, but he did. He did not look like he was joking, but I kept expecting a punch line. Instead, he started telling me how aliens from outer space were responsible for all sorts of accomplishments in the ancient world. He was convinced this was true; after all, he had learned about it on the History Channel.

This incident helped to heighten my awareness of all types of information and misinformation that are floating around. Sometimes it is hard to find truth in the midst of all the confusion. And, apparently, even intelligent, aware people are being fooled.

Are you ready to join me on this journey for truth? I believe we will have a fun and interesting time together as we explore the physical and supernatural worlds.

Who knows? You may never look at life the same way again.

Not Quite, Mr. Darwin

The heavens declare the glory of God; the skies proclaim the work of his hands.

Psalm 19:1 NIV

Let's begin our quest for answers by taking a look at the universe we live in. Perhaps this is putting the cart before the horse, but I want to start with Charles Darwin's brainchild, the theory of evolution.

Charles Darwin originally intended to become an Anglican priest, but he changed direction after developing a strong interest in the natural world. Five years traveling through South America and the Galápagos Islands allowed him to record observations about the development of life forms in isolated environments. These observations became the basis for his best-known work, *On the Origin of Species*.

Darwin proposed that all living creatures are descended from a small set of common ancestors. The survival of an organism, he believed, depends on its ability to adapt to its environment, a process he called "natural selection." Recognizing, in the words of author Francis Collins, "the potentially explosive nature of the argument,"[1] Darwin took the concept of natural selection to its logical conclusion, arguing in *The Descent of Man* that human beings themselves evolved through the same process.

When Darwin published *On the Origin of Species* in 1859, he tried hard not to offend people who believed in God:

I see no good reason why the views given in this volume should shock the religious feelings of anyone. . . . A celebrated author and divine has written to me that he "has gradually learned to see that it is just as noble a conception of the deity to believe that he created a few original forms capable of self-development into other and needful forms, as to believe that he required a fresh act of creation to supply the voids caused by the action of his laws."[2]

Mere pages later, Darwin concludes *On the Origin of Species* with these words:

There is grandeur in this view of life, with its several powers, having been originally breathed by the Creator into a few forms or into one; and that, whilst this planet has gone cycling on according to the fixed law of gravity, from so simple a beginning endless forms most beautiful and wonderful have been and are being evolved.[3]

Clearly Charles Darwin did not intend to start a war between science and religion. He did not feel that the Bible's account of creation was incompatible with what he had written in *On the Origin of Species.*

But most people did not see it that way. Although Darwin apparently did not mean for it to happen, most people seemed to think that the theory of evolution took God out of the equation. Darwin's disciples no longer had any need for an intelligent designer behind the creation and development of our universe. They believed all that was needed to create life was an accidental combination of just the right chemicals, favorable conditions and plenty of time.

Over the next 150 years, Darwin's theory became accepted as gospel. Those who questioned it were dismissed as kooks and dullards. A belief in evolution was an article of faith for anyone who wanted to teach science, from grade school all the way through graduate school.

Nearly a hundred years after publication of *On the Origin of Species*, two distinguished scientists named Stanley Miller and Harold Urey conducted an experiment that seemed to support the idea that life evolved or materialized or originated on its own. They tried to reconstruct—on a very small scale—the conditions that existed on earth when the first life appeared here by mixing water and several atmospheric gases to develop a primordial soup. They then sent an electric current coursing through the mixture. As a result, a number of important biological building blocks were formed, such as amino acids.

This experiment lent credence to the theory that, given enough time and the right conditions, life could spontaneously originate and later develop into the complexity of life we see today. Perhaps you have heard the analogy that if you put a bunch of monkeys in a cage with computers, given enough time, they would eventually turn out the entire works of Shakespeare. I have heard that type of thing said over and over to support the validity of evolution, and it is always presented not as a theory but as a solid fact—and most people seem to believe it. But is it true?

Shakespeare and the Monkeys

Philosopher Antony Flew was once one of the world's best-known atheists. In his last years, his continued study—especially of recent scientific discoveries—brought him to faith in God. He wrote of one experiment in which six monkeys in a cage were given a computer and allowed to have at it. After one month, the monkeys had produced fifty typed pages. How many complete English words (with a space on either side) had they produced?

Not one—not even *a* or *I*.[4]

Flew realized from this experiment that a divine design to the universe was more likely than he had thought. He was further persuaded by Gerald L. Schroeder, a Massachusetts Institute of Technology–trained scientist who has worked in both physics and biology. Schroeder noted that Shakespeare's famous sonnet "Shall I compare thee to a Summer's day?" is 488 letters long. Calculating the odds that random typing would produce the 488 letters of that sonnet in sequence is mathematically straightforward: You multiply 26 (the number of letters in the alphabet) times itself 488 times. This is on the order of 10 to the 690th power—meaning that you would have to try this random sequencing of letters 10-followed-by-690-zeros times to hit upon the correct combination.

This number is so astronomically high as to be impossible. There simply has not been enough time or matter in the universe (if matter represented individual letters) to produce just one of Shakespeare's sonnets by chance, much less the complexity of life. Schroeder concluded that "you will never get a sonnet by chance. . . . Yet the world just thinks the monkeys can do it every time."[5]

The moral of the story is simple: Do not believe everything you hear. Speaking of which, you may have heard that Albert Einstein, the greatest scientist of modern times, was an atheist. But Einstein himself denied this:

I'm not an atheist, and I don't think I can call myself a pantheist. We are in the position of a little child entering a huge library filled with books in many languages. The child knows someone must have written those books. It does not know how. It does not understand the languages in which they are written. The child dimly suspects a mysterious order in the arrangement of the books but doesn't know what it is. That, it seems to me, is the attitude of even the most intelligent human being toward God. We see the universe marvelously arranged and obeying certain laws but only dimly understand those laws. Our limited minds grasp the mysterious force that moves the constellations.[6]

Einstein also said,

I have never found a better expression than "religious" for this trust in the rational nature of reality and of its peculiar accessibility to the human mind. Where this trust is lacking, science degenerates into an uninspired procedure. . . . Everyone who is seriously engaged in the pursuit of science becomes convinced that the laws of nature manifest the existence of a spirit vastly superior to that of men, and one in the face of which we with our modest powers must feel humble.[7]

Believing that life on earth came together by chance is like believing that a strong wind blowing through a junkyard would eventually put together a top-of-the-line Mercedes. Does that not sound ridiculous? Remember that our universe, and the human body in particular, is much more complex than the latest breakthrough in automobile engineering.

On Behalf of Darwin

To be sure, there have been hundreds, even thousands, of discoveries that support many of Darwin's ideas.

Francis S. Collins, whom I quoted earlier, is a respected scientist and devout Christian. He led one of the greatest scientific endeavors of the 21st century—the Human Genome Project. Collins sees no reason why anyone should have to choose between the theory of evolution and the Bible's account of creation.

Dr. Collins does not see the theory of evolution as an enemy of faith, but rather as an ally, revealing God's power and creativity:

> For me, there is not a shred of disappointment or disillusionment in these discoveries about the nature of life—quite the contrary! How marvelous and intricate life turns out to be! . . . Evolution, as a mechanism, can be and must be true. But that says nothing about the nature of its author. For those who believe in God, there are reasons now to be more in awe, not less.[8]

Collins points out that the book of Genesis lists an order of creation that agrees with what Darwin believed. First came

20

vegetation of all kinds. Then fish and birds. These were followed by land animals—and finally human beings.

Read the creation account in the first chapter of Genesis, and you will also see that God said,

> "Let the land produce vegetation: seed-bearing plants and trees on the land that bear fruit with seed in it, according to their various kinds." And it was so. The land produced vegetation: plants bearing seed according to their kinds and trees bearing fruit with seed in it according to their kinds.
>
> Genesis 1:11–12 NIV

A bit further down, we read, "And God said, 'Let the land produce living creatures according to their kinds: livestock, the creatures that move along the ground, and the wild animals, each according to its kind.' And it was so" (Genesis 1:24 NIV).

There is a case to be made that the ground brought forth the living creatures, but it was responding to God's command.

How Did Consciousness Begin?

Despite the fact that it may be possible, at least in some ways, to square the Bible's account of creation with the teachings of Charles Darwin, there are at least three major problems with the theory of evolution:

1. It cannot explain how life began. While Dawin's theory of evolution may seem logical, it never explains how the chasm between nonlife and life was bridged.
2. It does not take into account the Bible's clear teaching that the creation of human beings was a special,

21

separate act. The Bible tells us that Adam and Eve did not gradually appear, over time, as the world evolved. Rather God took special care to create mankind in His own image: He "breathed into his nostrils a breath of life" (Genesis 2:7).

3. Evolution cannot answer another most intriguing question: *Where did consciousness come from?*

It is one thing to believe that a rudimentary form of life came from inanimate objects—from rocks, water, air, fire and so forth—but how did that "life" begin to think? Physical changes are one thing. The ability to think and reason is another matter entirely. This is where the real mystery begins.

If we are merely machines controlled by our brains, then where did our emotions come from? How did we learn to love our parents, our spouses, our children and our friends? How did we come to understand the difference between right and wrong, and why do we get a guilty conscience when we do something we know we should not do? Who or what told us we should not do it?

John Polkinghorne, who is both a theoretical physicist and Anglican priest, uses music to explain the difference between mere biological life and something deeper that goes to the core of who we are as human beings:

> The poverty of an objectivist account is made only too clear when we consider the mystery of music. From a scientific point of view, it is nothing but vibrations in the air, impinging on the eardrums and stimulating neural currents in the brain.
>
> How does it come about that this banal sequence of temporal activity has the power to speak to our hearts of an eternal beauty? The whole range of subjective experience, from

perceiving a patch of pink, to being enthralled by a performance of the Mass in B Minor, and on to the mystic's encounter with the ineffable reality of the One, all these truly human experiences are at the center of our encounter with reality, and they are not to be dismissed as epiphenomenal froth on the surface of a universe whose true nature is impersonal and lifeless.[9]

Antony Flew invites his readers to imagine a marble table and asks,

Do you think that given a trillion years or infinite time, this table could suddenly or gradually become conscious, aware of its surroundings, aware of its identity the same way you are? It is simply inconceivable that this would or could happen. And the same goes for any kind of matter. Once you understand the nature of matter, of mass-energy, you realize that, by its very nature it could never become "aware," never "think," never say, "I." But the atheist position is that, at some point in the history of the universe, the impossible and the inconceivable took place. . . . Returning to our table, we see why this is simply laughable.[10]

Charles Darwin himself admitted that he was challenged

by the extreme difficulty, or rather the impossibility of conceiving of this immense and wonderful universe, including man, with his capacity for looking far backwards and far into futurity, as the result of blind chance or necessity. When thus reflecting I feel compelled to look to a First Cause having an intelligent mind in some degree analogous to that of a man; and I deserve to be called a theist.[11]

In my book *A Rabbi Looks at the Afterlife*, I wrote about the philosopher John Locke, who asked what would happen if a prince and a cobbler suddenly exchanged consciousnesses one night while they were sleeping. When they woke up the next morning, would they be the men they were when they first went to sleep? The answer is yes; they would have the same bodies they had before. But would they be the same person? No—because each would now have the memories and consciousness of the other.

Personal identity, Locke argues, is not the same as having the same physical substance. There is something more that makes us who we truly are.

Our Intelligent Universe

Anyone who looks at our universe with an open mind can see the visible signs of divine design. From the immense complexity of the human body to the delicate balance of gravitational forces and atmosphere required for the survival of the earth to the incredible diversity of nature, the handiwork of a supreme intelligence is obvious.

We see this declared in the New Testament: "For since the creation of the world God's invisible qualities—his eternal power and divine nature—have been clearly seen, being understood from what has been made" (Romans 1:20).

According to Schroeder, we need look no further to see this apparent consciousness than our own bodies, far more complex and amazing than any machine conceived by human beings—to the point that the inner workings of our very cells inspire "almost a religious experience [of awe] even for a secular spectator."[12] Each cell, which he likens to circuits of a computer board—only more tightly packed—builds two thousand proteins every second. Each protein contains several hundred amino acids, which together contain thousands of atoms. As you can see, that is a mind-blowing amount of work happening every second inside of you, making the busiest factory in North America look like "Lazytown." Your body—and those of everyone else you know—has more than 37 *trillion* of these cells, moving with a precision that would turn a Broadway dance troupe's faces green with envy. Imagine 37 trillion cars flying at maximum speed on a series of complicated highways without a single mishap. Then just imagine that it all happened by chance. That there was no design or foresight involved at all.

I do not know about you, but to me the idea that our bodies or, for that matter, the entire universe came together by chance is starting to sound as absurd as the theory of spontaneous generation that was discredited by science in the 1800s. People once believed that maggots appearing in a rotten piece of meat had come to life from nothing; they had no understanding that maggots arose from microscopic fly eggs deposited when flies landed on the meat. Thanks to scientists like Louis Pasteur, we now understand that living organisms cannot be produced by nonliving things. Yet the theory of evolution sounds very much like spontaneous generation, if on a much longer time scale.

Earlier we considered the experiment of Miller and Urey that suggested that organic compounds necessary for life could have spontaneously formed in the conditions present on the early earth. But, as Francis Collins writes,

> Beyond this point, however, the details become quite sketchy. How could self-replicating information-carrying molecules assemble spontaneously from these compounds? DNA . . . seems an utterly improbable molecule to have

"just happened"—especially since DNA seems to possess no intrinsic means of copying itself.

. . . The profound difficulties in defining a convincing pathway for life's origin have led some scientists, most notably Francis Crick (who with James Watson discovered the DNA double helix), to propose that life forms must have arrived on Earth from outer space. . . . While this might solve the dilemma of life's appearance on Earth, it does nothing to resolve the ultimate question of life's origin, since it simply forces that astounding event to another time and place even further back.[13]

In discussing the improbability of the "coincidences that led to life and consciousness" following the big bang, Schroeder concludes, "From a ball of energy that turned into rocks and water, we get the consciousness of a thought. And all by random, unthinking reactions. Even to an atheist, this line of reasoning must seem a bit forced."[14]

As far back as 1983, researcher and author Jeremy Rifkin reported that the scientific world was beginning to look upon the entire universe as an intelligent organism. Scientific inquiry revealed the natural world responding in a way that was unexpected for an unintelligent system. For example, Rifkin reported that scientists took a few genes from an insect's leg. Then they removed one of the creature's antennas, grafted the leg genes into where the antenna had been, and waited to see what happened. If things went according to their expectations, the creature would sprout a leg on its head. After all, the grafted-in cells contained all the genetic information necessary to become a leg. But that is not what happened. Instead, those "leg genes" developed a new antenna. How?

Nothing in the genetic code of that leg should have given it the ability to become an antenna.

Yet, somehow, it seemed to "know" that an antenna was precisely what was needed.[15] Apparently, the universe is "smarter" than we knew. Once again, a super intelligence seems to be at work.

According to quantum physics, everything that exists in our universe is made up of information, from the grass in your front yard to the mountains, oceans and clouds in the sky. Quantum physicists have even discovered that some particles behave differently depending on whether they are being watched. They have also found that it is possible for two particles to occupy the same space at the same time. Newtonian physics says that is impossible. But it happens. Apparently, we are not living in the simple universe Newton—or Charles Darwin—believed in.

As he accepted the prestigious Templeton Prize, physicist Freeman Dyson said,

> Atoms are weird stuff, behaving like active agents rather than inert substances. They make unpredictable choices between alternative possibilities according to the laws of quantum mechanics. It appears that mind, as manifested by the capacity to make choices, is to some extent inherent in every atom. The universe is also weird, with its laws of nature that make it hospitable to the growth of mind. I do not make any clear distinction between mind and God. God is what mind becomes when it has passed beyond the scale of our comprehension.[16]

God and the Big Bang

I doubt there is any educated adult in the Western world who has not heard of the big bang theory, and I am not talking about the TV show. The big bang was the enormous explosion that formed our universe out of a speck of matter condensed into a space no bigger than the head of a pin.

There was a time when I thought of the big bang as just another scientific substitute for God. *Well, they can't say God created the universe,* I thought, *so they invented something called the "big bang."*

Not exactly.

The truth is that scientists once believed that our universe had always been here. They had no need for a creator because they did not think there had been a creation.

Then, as scientists often do when new information comes along, they changed their minds. It became apparent that our universe began at a specific date in history. There *had* been a creation, and, as far as science was concerned, that opened the door for belief in God. In other words, a creation cannot happen without a creator. And the big bang has God's fingerprints all over it.

Stephen Hawking, author of *A Brief History of Time* and subject of the movie *The Theory of Everything*, is known for his brilliant mind and his long, courageous battle against ALS (Lou Gehrig's disease). He is also known as an agnostic. But talking about the big bang, he says, "It would be very difficult to explain why the universe should have begun in just this way, except as the act of a God who intended to create beings just like us."[17]

Hawking is not the only brilliant scientist of the modern era who has talked openly about God. Freeman Dyson said, "The more I examine the universe and the details of its architecture, the more evidence I find that the universe in some sense might have known we were coming."[18]

Author Hugh Ross wrote in his book *The Creator and the Cosmos*,

Wherever we look in the realm of nature, we see evidence for God's design and exquisite care for His creatures. Whether we examine the cosmos on its largest scale or its tiniest, His handiwork is evident. Whether we work in disciplines where simplicity and rigor predominate (for example, mathematics, astronomy, and physics) or in disciplines where complexity and information predominate (for example, biochemistry, botany, and zoology), God's fingerprints are visible.[19]

There are many reasons why I believe our universe was carefully designed by a caring God. Consider our sun: If it were any larger it would burn too quickly to maintain life. Smaller, and no life could exist. If it were any redder or bluer, as many stars are, photosynthesis would be insufficient. If our earth were 2 percent closer or farther from the sun, all life would be destroyed. Here are some other "amazing coincidences" about the universe we live in:

- If the earth were not tilted at an angle of 23.5 degrees, there would be no seasons, leading to a drastic reduction in living space able to support human life and greater hunger among the population due to the lack of essential crops.
- If the earth's crust were ten feet thicker, there would be no oxygen in our atmosphere.
- If the oceans were just a few feet deeper, all carbon dioxide and oxygen would be absorbed into them, destroying all life on earth.

According to a physicist named Chet Raymo,

> If, one second after the Big Bang, the ratio of the density of
> the universe to its expansion rate had differed from its as-
> sumed value by only one part in ten to the fifteenth power
> (that's 1 followed by fifteen zeroes), the universe would have
> either quickly collapsed upon itself or ballooned so rapidly
> that stars and galaxies could not have condensed from the
> primal matter. . . . The coin was flipped into the air ten to
> the fifteenth power times, and it came down on its edge but
> once. If all the grains of sand on all the beaches of the Earth
> were possible universes—that is, universes consistent with
> the laws of physics as we know them—and only one of those
> grains of sand were a universe that allowed for the existence
> of intelligent life, then that one grain of sand is the universe
> we inhabit.[20]

We do not have to stop there—we could go on to talk
about the fine structure constant,[21] the way water appears
designed to support molecular reactions necessary for life,[22]
the improbable stability of our solar system[23] and the "ex-
ceptionally benign luminosity stability" of our sun,[24] all
of which make life on earth possible. The more we learn
about the universe, the more it seems clear that we are not
here by chance.

Frederic B. Burnham, a science historian, says that the
idea that God created the universe is now "a more respect-
able hypothesis at this point in time than at any time in the
last hundred years."[25]

And the late astrophysicist Fred Hoyle was so amazed
by the discoveries about the universe that were being made
toward the end of his life that he admitted his atheism had
been "greatly shaken."[26]

Dr. Hoyle, who taught at Cambridge University for almost thirty years, also said, "If one proceeds directly and straight-forwardly in this matter, without being deflected by a fear of incurring the wrath of scientific opinion, one arrives at the conclusion that biomaterials with their amazing measure of order must be the outcome of intelligent design. No other possibility I have been able to think of."[27]

And again, "The notion that not only the biopolymer but the operating program of a living cell could be arrived at by chance in a primordial organic soup here on the earth is evidently nonsense of a high order."[28]

The Fingerprints of God

Have you ever heard anyone say that only an uneducated, unscientific mind would entertain the possibility of "intelligent design"?

Obviously, that is not the truth. God's fingerprints are all around us. The closer we look, the easier it is to see them. Antony Flew quotes physiologist and Nobel Laureate George Wald, who argued that "we choose to believe the impossible: that life arose spontaneously by chance."[29] Wald also argued for the idea that a "preexisting mind" was responsible for the universe:

How is it that, with so many other apparent options, we are in a Universe that possesses just that peculiar nexus of properties that breeds life? It has occurred to me lately—I must confess with some shock at first to my scientific sensibilities—that both questions might be brought into some degree of congruence. This is with the assumption that mind, rather than emerging as a late outgrowth in the evolution of

31

life, has existed always, as the matrix, the source and condition of physical reality—that the stuff of which physical reality is composed is mind-stuff. It is mind that has composed a physical Universe that breeds life, and so eventually evolves creatures that know and create: science-, art-, and technology-making animals.[30]

Of Wald's perspective, Flew says, "This, too, is my conclusion. The only satisfactory explanation of such 'end-directed, self-reciprocating life' as we see on earth is an infinitely intelligent Mind."[31]

Roy Abraham Varghese, co-author of Flew's book *There Is a God* and founder of the Institute for Metascientific Research, contends,

It's simply inconceivable that any material matrix or field can generate agents who think and act. Matter cannot produce conceptions and perceptions. A force field does not plan or think. So at the level of reason and everyday experience, we become immediately aware that the world of living, conscious, thinking beings has to originate in a living Source—a Mind.[32]

Personally, I believe that if you are still looking for a reason why we are here on this planet—and how we got here—there is no better explanation than the one found in the Bible:

In the beginning God created the heavens and the earth. Now the earth was chaos and waste, darkness was on the surface of the deep, and the Ruach Elohim was hovering upon the surface of the water. Then God said, "Let there be light!" and there was light. God saw that the light was good. . . . So there was evening and there was morning—one day.

Then God said, "Let there be an expanse in the midst of the water! Let it be for separating water from water." So God made the expanse and it separated the water that was below the expanse from the water that was over the expanse. And it happened so. God called the expanse "sky." So there was evening and there was morning—a second day.

Then God said, "Let the water below the sky be gathered to one place. Let the dry ground appear." And it happened so. God called the dry ground "land," and the collection of the water He called "seas." . . . The land brought forth grass, green plants yielding seed, each according to its species, and trees making fruit with the seed in it, each according to its species. And God saw that it was good. So there was evening and there was morning—a third day.

Then God said, "Let lights in the expanse of the sky be for separating the day from the night. . . . Then God made the two great lights—the greater light for dominion over the day, and the lesser light as well as the stars for dominion over the night. . . . So there was evening and there was morning—a fourth day.

Then God said, "Let the waters swarm with swarms of living creatures! Let flying creatures fly above the land across the expanse of the sky." . . . So there was evening and there was morning—a fifth day.

Then God said, "Let the land bring forth living creatures according to their species—livestock, crawling creatures and wild animals, according to their species." And it happened so. . . .

And God saw that it was good.

Then God said, "Let Us make man in Our image, after Our likeness! Let them rule over the fish of the sea, over the flying creatures of the sky, over the livestock, over the whole earth, and over every crawling creature that crawls on the land." God created humankind in His image, in the image of God He created him, male and female He created them.

God blessed them and God said to them, "Be fruitful and multiply, fill the land, and conquer it. Rule over the fish of the sea, the flying creatures of the sky, and over every animal that crawls on the land."

Genesis 1:1–10, 12–14, 16, 19–20, 23–28

3

The Invisible World

One phenomenon that consistently took place was a spirit identifying itself to us before we received a message. This was done by the spirit making a sign or spelling its name. There was one spirit, however, that never did this. Instead, we would all feel an uneasy, foreboding presence in the room, and it would become cold. We would feel overshadowed by this spirit and it would spell out a message very deliberately and slowly. The message was always the same: "All is dark. Pray for us."

Ben Alexander[1]

"There's no such thing as ghosts."
Did your mom ever say that to you when you were a kid? Mine did. Especially when I had watched a movie that was a little bit too scary for me and I was having trouble falling asleep.

Most of us parents have probably said it to our children at one time or another. But do we really believe it?

This book is about searching for answers to some of life's most important questions, so let me ask you another one.

Have you ever *seen* a ghost?

An angel?

A UFO?

If so, you have lots of company.

According to a 2009 survey conducted by the Pew Research Center, almost one in five American adults (18 percent) say they have seen or been in the presence of a ghost. A whopping 29 percent reported they have felt in touch with the dead![2]

Millions more claim to have seen unidentified flying objects, including former President Jimmy Carter. "I don't laugh at people anymore when they say they've seen UFOs," Carter said later. "I've seen one myself."[3]

I have no doubt that many people see spirits, strange lights in the sky and strange phenomena because they want to. They hunger for an encounter with the supernatural world, so they get one.

Sometimes, that encounter may be the result of nothing more than an overactive imagination. It may be the result of a scam—these days there seems to be a con artist behind every tree. Other times, I am afraid something far more sinister may be taking place.

After all, the Bible warns us that "even satan masquerades as an angel of light" (2 Corinthians 11:14).

Now, I certainly cannot blame people for wanting to know that there is more to life than the daily grind, getting up every day to go to work and coming home just to do it again the next. I am convinced there *is* more to life, though I did not always think this was so. My focus was on becoming a successful businessman and making as much money as I could.

That changed when I went to college and started to experiment with drugs; two years later, I had a supernatural encounter of my own—with Yeshua HaMashiach, Jesus the Messiah. I have told the story in detail in my previous books, *A Rabbi Looks at Jesus of Nazareth* and *A Rabbi Looks at the Last Days*, so I will not go into it again here. I will just say that one moment I was not really sure that God existed or that, if He did, He had any great purpose for my life. The next moment, I was certain of both.

In my case, I was definitely *not* looking for a supernatural encounter with God. My life was going along quite well, thank you. I did not feel like I needed anything more. While I believed that there was a God and knew by this time that a supernatural realm existed, it could get along just fine without me. Then a hand reached out of the invisible world, took me by the shoulder and changed everything.

I happen to believe that a lot of hands are reaching out to us, and if we are not extremely careful, we just might grab hold of the wrong one.

Mark was suffering from anxiety and stress. He was not popular and suffered a great deal of parental rejection. Though bright, he was sickly looking and lonely.

Life felt meaningless and stressful. Then a friend suggested he try an Eastern form of meditation. He said it was a great way to find peace and acceptance and offload stress, so Mark tried it.

Almost immediately, he began to feel better. Meditation worked, and Mark discovered that he was good at it, able to quickly shut out the noise of the outside world. He was peaceful.

Then, one day, when Mark had gone deeper into meditation than ever before, something frightening happened.

Mark found himself face-to-face with a hideous monster. It seemed to mock him, threatening to take control of his life and daring him to stop it. Was it a vision? Was it real? He was not sure, but the impact of the creature's appearance jolted Mark back to reality. He never tried meditation again.

Asked why the creature revealed itself, Mark says, "I have no idea. Maybe they figured I was so far gone that they had me, so they had nothing to lose by revealing themselves to me."

"Themselves?"

"The ones who are behind it all. Satan and his demons."[4]

Peggy was driving down a street in Denver, Colorado, at about 10:30 one night, when she heard the roar of an airliner passing overhead, making its approach to Stapleton International Airport.

Wait a minute! The aircraft seemed much too low! Was it going to crash? She was afraid it was going to smash into the top of the car.

She swerved to the side of the road, peered out the window and got the shock of her life. That was no airplane. Peggy recalls that it was a "dome-shaped" craft, and she could see someone moving around inside.

Suddenly, she received a telepathic message, "Don't forget us," and then the huge craft floated away. Soon after this incident, Peggy began receiving more messages. On the advice of her "alien" friends, Peggy and her husband moved from Denver to California and began conducting regular classes in which she and her friends tried to "raise the vibrations of the world."[5]

Kendall was on her way home when a pickup truck smashed into the side of her car, killing its driver instantly. Momentarily unconscious, the sixteen-year-old woke to a touch on her shoulder. A woman with red hair was looking in through what was left of the passenger side window. Kendall knew the lady could not have touched her, but she felt a strong spiritual connection between them. Somehow, at that moment, she knew she was going to be all right. Then the paramedics arrived, and Kendall never saw her again. In fact, *no one* saw the woman, including the only witness to the accident that investigators found. But everyone was astounded to see Kendall walk away uninjured.

"My mom says it was my guardian angel," Kendall testifies. "If I would have died that day, I probably would be headed for hell, but thanks for God's grace. He saved me and gave me another chance."[6]

Angels Among Us

Do angels really exist? If so, who or what are they? What is their purpose in this world?

The Bible mentions angels more than three hundred times, so anyone who accepts the Bible as true must believe in angels. The Bible also tells us that angels are God's messengers, and there are many examples of this within the Scriptures. The angel Gabriel brought the message to Mary that she was going to give birth to the Son of God (Luke 1:26–38). He was also dispatched to Zechariah to tell him that he and his wife, Elizabeth, were going to become the parents of John the Baptist (Luke 1:11–20). We also find, in Luke 2:8–14, that angels announced the birth of Yeshua to shepherds watching over their flocks.

Over the last fifteen years or so, the world has become fascinated with angels. They are everywhere—on television, on the big screen and online. Go into any bookstore and you are likely to find dozens of books about them. There are so many different teachings about angels that it can be hard to cut through the clutter to find out what is real and what is nothing more than imagination gone wild.

It is no surprise that angels are this popular, especially in these uncertain times, when terrorism, war and violence seem to be all around us. Angels are seen as loving and self-less. They speak to us of another world that is better than this one. They let us know that God is alive and well and that He still has everything under control, even in the midst of the chaos swirling around us. Furthermore, angels do not ask for a commitment or demand anything of us. People of many different faiths believe in angels, including Muslims. The angels that are popular today do not seem to judge us or care what we believe, and that is a good thing, right? Or maybe not.

The problem for us is that not all angels are to be trusted. Satan himself was once an angel, and, as I mentioned earlier, the Bible tells us that he can transform himself into an angel of light (2 Corinthians 11:14). Although the Bible does not give us many details, there are at least two passages that indicate that Satan convinced one third of the angels to join him in a rebellion against God. Their defeat is certain, but they have not yet given up. Revelation 12:7–9 says,

And war broke out in heaven, Michael and his angels making war against the dragon. The dragon and his angels fought, but they were not strong enough, and there was no longer any place for them in heaven. And the great dragon was thrown down—the ancient serpent, called the devil and satan, who deceives the whole world. He was thrown down to the earth, and his angels were thrown down with him.

And Isaiah 14:12–17 tells us,

How you have fallen from heaven, O brightstar, son of the dawn! How you are cut down to the earth, you who made the nations prostrate! You said in your heart: "I will ascend to heaven, I will exalt my throne above the stars of God. I will sit upon the mount of meeting, in the uttermost parts of the north. I will ascend above the high places of the clouds—I will make myself like Elyon." Yet you will be brought down to Sheol, to the lowest parts of the Pit. Those who see you will stare at you, reflecting on what has become of you: "Is this the one who shook the earth, who made kingdoms tremble, who made the world a wilderness and destroyed its cities, who never opened the house of his prisoners?"

Most Bible teachers believe that Satan's fallen angels became the demons that Jesus often battles within the pages of the New Testament. They may come to us pretending to be angels of light, ambassadors from outer space, loved ones who have died or wearing many other disguises.

Many voices are calling to us, and we all must be very careful about who we listen to. In Galatians 1:8, the apostle Paul writes, "But even if we (or an angel from heaven) should announce any 'good news' to you other than what we have proclaimed to you, let that person be cursed!"

41

Angels of Deception

Did you know that Muhammad started the Muslim religion after a visit from an angel? Islam teaches that Muhammad was in the habit of going to the cave of Hira, a few miles from Mecca, to pray and worship God. He loved the solitude and sometimes spent days alone in the cave before returning to his family.

On one of these occasions, Muhammad reported that the angel Gabriel appeared to him and commanded, "Read!"

Muhammad was an uneducated man who had never learned to read or write. When he told the angel he could not read, the angel grabbed Muhammad and embraced him so tightly that he almost lost consciousness.

Then he let go and again commanded Muhammad to read.

Muhammad protested a second time that he did not know how to read, and a second time Gabriel squeezed the breath out of him. Then he released him and commanded him a third time to read.

This time, Muhammad opened his mouth and began reciting verses of what was to become the Quran. Thus, the Muslim religion was born. Shortly after this, Gabriel appeared to Muhammad a second time and commissioned him to begin the work of publicly serving as Allah's prophet.

Joseph Smith is another "prophet" who claimed that he was visited by an angel before he began writing—or rather, translating—the Book of Mormon.

Smith claimed that when he was seventeen years old, the angel Moroni appeared to him and told him that he had been chosen by God to restore the true Christian church, which had been corrupted over the centuries. (This, by the way, is very similar to the assignment "Gabriel" reportedly gave to

Muhammad.) The angel directed Smith to a nearby hillside, where he would be shown where to dig to find golden tablets covered with hieroglyphs. Smith did as the angel directed, and, sure enough, the tablets were exactly where the angel said they would be.

Smith took them home, where he was given the supernatural ability to translate the hieroglyphs into English. When he was finished, Moroni appeared again and took the miraculous tablets back to heaven with him.

Is it true that Muhammad and Joseph Smith were visited by angels? There is no way we can know for certain. But if they were, the two angels did not agree on much of anything. There is no way to reconcile the Book of Mormon with the Quran.

They do not match up with the Bible, either. The Book of Mormon, for example, teaches that the God who rules the earth is not the God of the entire universe. There are many civilizations throughout space, and each has its own god to worship. In fact, all of us have the potential to become gods someday and rule over our own planets. To be certain, this is not what the Bible teaches—in either the Old or New Testament. And the Quran teaches that Jesus was an important prophet but denies that He is the Son of God, or that He went to the cross to save us from our sins. If the Bible is the standard by which all other books are to be judged—and I believe with my whole heart that it is—then the Book of Mormon and the Quran do not measure up.

The lesson to be learned is that if an angel appears to you and brings you a message, you do not have to believe it. But how do you judge? How can you tell if he is on God's side? Here are a few things to keep in mind:

- God's angels will never tell you anything that is contrary to His Word as contained in the Bible.

- An angel from God is never willing to accept the praise or worship of human beings (see Colossians 2:18 and Revelation 19:10). True angels always seek to bring glory to God and His Son, Jesus, the Messiah. The only exceptions appear in the Old Testament, in which the "angel of the Lord," I believe, was God Himself (see Genesis 18 and Judges 6).

- God's angels understand that we are all powerless apart from God. An angel who tells you that you have the power within you to bring about your own salvation is not to be trusted.

Real or Imagination?

In the early 1970s, a group of paranormal researchers decided to try to "create" their own spirit. Members of the Toronto Society for Psychical Research imagined a character and tried to get him to manifest himself in a séance.[7]

They chose the name Philip Aylesford and, like novelists fleshing out a character, wrote his backstory. It was decided that Philip had been born in 1624 in England, became a military hero at a very young age and was knighted at sixteen. The researchers also decided that Philip had been unhappily married to a woman named Dorothea but fell in love with a Gypsy girl who was condemned to death for practicing witchcraft. In despair, Philip committed suicide at age thirty. An artist even painted a picture of Philip— a handsome, noble-looking man who, remember, never existed.

Then it was time to try and contact him "on the other side." After months of séances, one day they heard loud rapping sounds when they called out Philip's name. The "ghost" had made his first appearance. The members of the group kept their hands visible so all could see that they were not making the rapping noises.

Philip continued to show up every time the group got together. They asked him questions about himself, and he would answer by tapping yes or no on the table. His answers always agreed with his backstory, and sometimes he added details to it.

At times Philip responded to singing by bouncing the table up and down in time to the music. The researchers reported that the table might playfully chase people around. On one occasion, it became stuck in a doorway after trying to follow one person out of the room.

Philip became a sensation and seemed to enjoy the spotlight. His friends and their table appeared on Toronto City Television in front of a live audience. Philip responded with loud rapping noises when the show's moderator called to him, and then the table bounced up and down as if alive. He answered questions from members of the audience by banging out his answers in the usual way. Later, he showed up, right on cue, for the filming of a documentary.

The only thing Philip could not deal with was a lack of belief. When a member of the Toronto group told him, "We only made you up, you know," Philip fell silent, almost as if he were sulking. It was only after members of the group redoubled their efforts to believe in him that he resumed his tricks.

Who was Philip? Was he merely a manifestation of the power of human thought—a trick of the subconscious mind?

Or was something more going on? Is it possible that a supernatural entity had been fooled into thinking that Philip had been a real person? Had he, or it, assumed Philip's personality in an attempt to make the researchers believe they had made contact with a disembodied human spirit? And, if so, what *was* this supernatural entity?

Let me give you a possible answer from C. S. Lewis, author of many classic books such as *Mere Christianity*, *The Problem of Pain* and The Chronicles of Narnia series.

In *The Screwtape Letters*, Lewis presents a series of letters full of advice from an older demon, Uncle Screwtape, to his young nephew, Wormwood. Among this advice is a list of three ways that demons can manipulate human beings:

1. Get them to think too much about demons.
2. Get them to completely ignore demons and refuse to even consider that they exist.
3. Get them to believe in a neutral force that is neither good nor evil.

On the third point, Screwtape writes, "If once we can produce our perfect work—the Materialist Magician, the man, not using, but veritably worshipping what he vaguely calls 'Forces' while denying the existence of 'spirits'—then the end of the war will be in sight."[8]

4

Ghosts and the Bible

There are beings "out there" anxious and ready
to communicate with us any time we are willing
to open our minds to them. Sometimes they present themselves as angels. Other times as beings
from other planets. And on still other occasions
as the disembodied spirits of loved ones who have
died. But I believe these voices "whispering in the
wind" come from none of these places.

Bill Myers[1]

I am not the sort of person who believes every "weird"
story I hear.

I am a natural-born "doubter." Show me the proof, and
then I will believe you. That is exactly what happened to me
in my spiritual pilgrimage. My encounter with the Lord was
followed by a desire to read the Scriptures for myself. When
I did, I found prophecy after prophecy about the Messiah,

written hundreds of years before Yeshua was even born. Prophecies that clearly pointed to Him as the Messiah. In the Scriptures—my own Jewish Scriptures, which we Jews claim to be our Holy Writings even though most of us have never read them (myself included, to that point)—I found my proof.

I tend to think that most stories about ghosts, demons and such are like mirages that disappear when you get close to them. Have you ever wasted your time watching one of those shows on cable TV about the search for Bigfoot? Every time they cut to a commercial, they promise to be "right back" with something really exciting. But they never do. They can keep you on the edge of your seat for an hour without ever showing you a thing—which means, of course, that they do not really *have* anything exciting to show you.

In the early 1970s, a man named Frank Smyth decided to make up a ghost story, get it published in a magazine and see what sort of response it got. He wrote a story about the ghost of a clergyman that haunted a house in London. The article even included the address of the house so readers could check it out if they wanted to.

Many of them wanted to. Responses came pouring in from people who claimed they had seen the ghost. Some gave vivid descriptions of the man, right down to the clerical collar he wore.

When Smyth had the magazine print a retraction, admitting that the story was fabricated, many readers refused to believe it. They insisted that they had seen the clergyman walking around the grounds of his house or looking out the window, and nobody was going to make them believe otherwise. One of the people who wrote letters to the magazine insisted that Smyth must have written the story under the influence of the ghost without realizing it.[2]

Some people will believe everything.

And yet, there *are* stories that hold up under the closest scrutiny. I have to admit that since I have been traveling around the world for my ministry with Jewish Voice—especially into remote areas of Africa and Asia—I have come to believe more strongly that there are supernatural forces at work in this world of ours, and that they are on both sides of the battle between good and evil. You cannot deny that demons exist after you have grappled with them head-on!

At the beginning of chapter 3, we noted that 18 percent of Americans say they have seen a ghost. That is more than 54 million men, women and children. Can that many people be mistaken about what they have seen? It seems unlikely. The sheer numbers lead us to think that *something real is going on out there.*

Besides, Yeshua Himself believed in demons. He believed in them because He had many confrontations with them—and it seems to me that this is a good reason why we should believe in them, too. Take this story from the book of Mark:

> As soon as Yeshua got out of the boat, a man from the graveyard with an unclean spirit met Him. He lived among the tombs, and no one could restrain him anymore, even with a chain. For he had often been bound with shackles and chains, but the chains had been ripped apart by him and the shackles broken. No one was strong enough to tame him.
>
> And through it all, night and day, at the graveyard and in the mountains, he kept screaming and gashing himself with stones.

When he saw Yeshua from a distance, he ran and bowed down before Him. Crying out with a loud voice, he said, "What's between You and me, Yeshua, Ben El Elyon? I'm warning you, in the name of God, do not torment me!"

For Yeshua had said to him, "Come out of the man, you unclean spirit!" Then Yeshua began questioning him, "What is your name?" And he answered, "My name is Legion, for we are many." He kept begging Him not to send them out of the country.

Now a large herd of pigs was feeding on the hillside nearby. The unclean spirits urged Him, saying, "Send us to the pigs, so we may enter them."

So Yeshua gave them permission. The unclean spirits came out and entered the pigs. And the herd, about two thousand in number, rushed down the cliff and were drowned in the sea.

Mark 5:2–13

Spirits Through the Ages

Spirits have been around for millennia. Or, more accurately, a *belief* in spirits has been around for millennia. References to ghosts are found in ancient writings from Mesopotamia and Egypt. They have always been thought to be spirits of people who have died. In many cultures, ghosts are associated with places or events that were especially important to a person in his or her lifetime. For instance, an apparition may be seen walking through the woods he loved or gazing out the window of the house she lived in for thirty years.

Jewish folktales are also full of stories about spirits, most of whom are known as *dybbuks*. According to Jewish mythology, the dybbuk is afraid or unable to move on to the next level of existence. This may be because he or she lived a wicked life and is trying to escape the punishment waiting in the next world—or it may be that the spirit has unfinished business in this one. If the spirit is that of a righteous person who has lingered to serve as a guide to people here, it is called a *maggid*, rather than a dybbuk.

Apparently, Yeshua's disciples believed in spirits. When Jesus came to them walking on the water, "they thought He was a ghost and cried out—for they all saw Him and were terrified. But immediately, He spoke to them. He said, 'Take courage! I am. Do not be afraid'" (Mark 6:49–50).

Yeshua could have told them there was no such thing as spirits, but He did not.

Something similar happened when He appeared to the disciples after His resurrection:

> While they were speaking of these things, Yeshua Himself stood in the midst of them and said, "Shalom Aleichem!" But they were startled and terrified, thinking they were seeing a ghost. Then He said to them, "Why are you so shaken? And why do doubts arise in your heart? Look at My hands and My feet—it is I Myself! Touch Me and see! For a spirit doesn't have flesh and bones, as you see I have."
>
> Luke 24:36–39

In the New International Version, that last line is translated, "a ghost does not have flesh and bones, as you see I have."

I acknowledge that this book is not a tutorial on the existence of spirits, but it is interesting to me that Yeshua's words may be seen as an acknowledgment that supernatural beings of some sort do exist.

The Ghost in the Bible

There is at least one "ghost story" to be found in the Bible, in 1 Samuel 28. At the time, Israel was about to go to war against the Philistines, which was not at all unusual. Saul, the king of Israel, had led his nation through many wars. He was a battle-hardened soldier who did not scare easily. But this time, the Bible says that when King Saul saw the Philistine army, terror filled his heart. There were a couple of reasons for this. First of all, Saul's longtime mentor, the prophet Samuel—the man who had anointed him king—was dead. Second, when Saul sought God's advice, the Lord did not respond. Saul needed reassurance and direction but was unable to get either.

He had always known that he could not lose as long as he was on God's side, but now it seemed that God had deserted him—and neither did he have the blessing of the great prophet.

For this reason, even though Saul knew that God had expressly forbidden consulting a spirit medium, that is what he decided to do. In disguise he visited a medium who lived in the village of Endor and asked her to summon Samuel from the grave. At first, the woman was suspicious. She did not recognize the king, but she was afraid he might be setting her up. But when "Saul vowed to her by ADONAI saying, 'As ADONAI lives, no punishment will come on you for this thing'" (1 Samuel 28:10), the woman agreed to "call up" Samuel, as Saul had requested. When she "saw" Samuel, she cried out with a loud shriek and said to the king, "Why have you deceived me? You are Saul!" (verse 12).

Bible commentators are not sure how she suddenly realized she was dealing with Saul. Some suggest it was because she was not really able to contact the dead. She was a charlatan who made her living by deceiving gullible people. When she saw that she had actually been able to summon a spirit this time, she knew that she was in the presence of the king. Others say that when she saw Samuel, she recognized him and knew that only the king would have the authority to summon him from the dead. We do not know for certain which is correct, or if there is some other reason why the woman suddenly realized that she was with the king.

Either way, Saul urged her to describe what she saw. "I see a godlike being coming up from the earth," she said. "An old man is coming up, and he is wrapped with a robe" (verses 13–14).

The Bible continues,

> Then Saul knew that it was Samuel, so he bowed down and prostrated himself with his face to the ground.
>
> Samuel said to Saul, "Why have you disturbed me by bringing me up?"
>
> "I'm in great distress," Saul answered. "The Philistines are waging war against me, and God has turned away from me—He doesn't answer me anymore, whether by prophets or by dreams. So I called you up to tell me what I should do."
>
> Samuel said, "So why ask me, since ADONAI has turned away from you and become your adversary? Now ADONAI has done for Himself just as He foretold through me—ADONAI has torn the kingship out of your hand and has given it to another fellow, to David. Since you did not obey the voice of ADONAI and did not execute His fierce wrath on Amalek, so ADONAI has done this to you today. Moreover, ADONAI will also give the Israelites who are with you into the hand of the Philistines. Tomorrow you and your sons will be with me! Yes, ADONAI will give the army of Israel into the hand of the Philistines."
>
> 1 Samuel 28:14–19

Everything happened exactly the way "the ghost" of Samuel said it would. The Israelites were defeated, Saul and his sons were killed and the throne passed into the hands of David. But that does not mean the medium had any special powers, or that she was able to predict the future. For some reason, God allowed Saul to hear from Samuel in this strange way.

This is an admittedly peculiar Scripture, and it has spurred a lot of debate. Some Bible scholars maintain that God would not have allowed a medium to summon the spirit of Samuel, so he was not really there. Others say that the Bible never hints that it was anyone but "the real Samuel" who spoke to Saul, so it must have been him.

Either way, the story ends badly for Saul. And it indicates that the ancient Israelites did believe that life goes on beyond the grave. (We will talk more about this in an upcoming chapter on heaven and hell.)

Voices from Beyond

Loved ones, do not believe every spirit, but test the spirits to see if they are from God. For many false prophets have gone out into the world. You know the Ruach Elohim [Holy Spirit] by this—every spirit that acknowledges that Messiah Yeshua has come in human flesh is from God, but every spirit that does not acknowledge Yeshua is not from God.

1 John 4:1–3

Testing spirits is a recurring theme of this chapter. Many voices are competing for our attention; some of those voices come from God, have our best interests at heart and are telling the truth. Other voices are lying to us for some reason—perhaps

54

because they want to destroy us. Whether they claim to be angels, ghosts, aliens or loved ones who have departed, some of these voices seem to know an awful lot about us. Their intimate knowledge seems to validate their claims of who they are.

But why is the Bible so insistent that God's people are not supposed to attempt communication with the dead? Deuteronomy 18:10–12 says,

> There must not be found among you anyone who makes his son or daughter pass through the fire, or a fortune-teller, soothsayer, omen reader, or sorcerer, or one who casts spells, or a medium, a spiritist, or one who calls up the dead. For whoever does these things is an abomination to ADONAI, and because of these abominations ADONAI your God is driving them out from before you.

Leviticus 19:31 echoes this: "Do not turn to those who are mediums or to soothsayers. Do not seek them out to be defiled by them. I am ADONAI your God." This is reinforced in the next chapter: "The soul that turns to mediums or to soothsayers, prostituting himself with them, I will set My face against that soul and will cut him off from among his people" (Leviticus 20:6).

Could it be that God knows this is one of Satan's most effective tools for bringing people into spiritual bondage?

Ben Alexander is founder of ESP Ministries (Exposing Satan's Power). Born into a Jewish family in England, Alexander became involved in spiritualism as a young man, after his mother and father died. He desperately wanted to know that his parents were still alive on "the other side," and he began seeking contact with them. He soon became an adept medium, delivering poignant messages from beyond.

Alexander recalls,

There was one thing that happened rather often and always disturbed me. We always had a Bible in the room [during séances]. Frequently it would rise off the table [and] then fly through the air and smash against the wall. One time a materialized spirit picked it up, peered into it very closely, and then threw it clear across the room. Since I believed that we were doing God's will, this was hard to understand. Whenever this happened the spirits would say that an evil spirit had gotten through and that it would not happen again. But it continued.[3]

On a trip to America, where he hoped to start a spiritualist organization, Alexander and his wife, Miranda, came to know Yeshua. That was in 1964. He renounced his work as a medium and has spent the last fifty-plus years warning of the dangers of spiritualism and other occult practices. He no longer believes that those messages came from departed friends and loved ones but rather from a more sinister source. He writes,

Satan has an uncanny knack of knowing many things about us. . . . At spiritualist meetings the medium will sometimes go straight to a person and tell him the full name of a dead relative, how the relative died and very intimate details about the individual and the dead person. It is no wonder people become convinced they are receiving messages from dead loved ones.[4]

When this belief is carried to the extreme, the consequences are ghastly. On March 26, 1997, police entering a mansion outside of San Diego, California, found a disturbing sight they will never forget. Inside the home lay 39 bodies, victims of the worst mass suicide ever carried out on American soil.

The dead men and women wore dark clothes and Nike sneakers. Almost all of them had their heads covered by plastic bags. Many had tags attached to them with the message "Heaven's Gate Away Team."

Authorities determined that the victims were members of the Heaven's Gate cult, founded by Marshall Applewhite and his partner, Bonnie Nettles. Applewhite's body was in the house. Nettles had "left her broken-down vehicle behind" (died) in 1985.

Applewhite had convinced his followers that a spaceship was coming to earth to take them to a higher level of existence. The spaceship, supposedly hidden from view behind the comet Hale-Bopp, was piloted by Nettles. In order to board the spaceship, the members of Heaven's Gate would have to leave all attachments to earth behind—including their bodies. In other words, they had to commit suicide. It sounds completely absurd, and it was. But 39 people believed it so absolutely that they freely consumed a fatal mixture of phenobarbital and vodka, knowing their companions would place plastic bags over their heads to ensure their suffocation. Terrible things can happen to us when we believe a lie.

By the way, if you go online to heavensgate.com, you'll find a fully functioning website hailing the arrival of Hale-Bopp and explaining that the members of Heaven's Gate are about to move on to a higher level of existence. There is even an invitation to send emails. But don't bother. Nobody is around to answer them. How tragic that those who believe they are on the road to enlightenment are often, instead, on the path to destruction.

Who Is Talking to You?

As we have already discussed in this chapter, many voices are whispering in the air around us, vying for our attention. Can we trust any voice that speaks to us from "beyond the grave"? Absolutely not.

But that does not mean that *every* supernatural voice is evil. Jack Deere, who was once convinced that God would not speak to anyone today apart from His Words recorded in the Bible, now feels quite differently about it. He is now convinced that God is still speaking to those who are willing to listen to Him, but that He never says anything that contradicts the Bible.

> Too much of the church today has more confidence in Satan's ability to deceive us than in God's ability to speak to us and lead us. There is a vast difference between the voice of God and the voice of Satan, and there are a number of scriptural safeguards to keep the sincere Christian from confusing the two.[5]

The Strange Story of Bill

In the early 1970s, Bill Fogarty and some other students at the University of Indiana developed an interest in the occult. They met weekly to talk about it, and though they were not prone to hallucinations, they began to experience things they could not account for—lights in the sky, heavy breathing and the like.

Unfazed, the students felt proud to be singled out for such experiences. But then the encounters grew violent: One member was slapped across the face by an unseen hand and kept awake at night by a vicious pounding noise. Others reported radios and televisions suddenly switching on when nobody was there. Some awoke during the night to find strangers standing by their beds. They had an uneasy feeling of being followed. One said he had been "teleported"—one minute, he was in his apartment; the next, he was in the woods, with no idea how he got there.

Was it a case of paranoia gone wild? It seemed unlikely— the young men considered themselves to be in good shape physically, mentally and emotionally. They were not easily scared. But they were so frightened now that they slept with guns within arm's reach.

It did not take long for the five friends to go separate ways. Two dropped out of school within weeks of graduation. One went deeper into the occult. Another became a born-again Christian. Looking back, Fogarty concluded that they had "tapped in to" some sort of energy—a natural force that had always been present on the earth.[6] But what natural force teleports people across town, slaps them in the face, turns appliances on or causes a loud pounding in the walls that keeps people awake at night?

What really happened to Bill and his friends?

Remember Ben Alexander, the former medium who now believes that "messages" from departed loved ones are actually from demonic entities masquerading as those loved ones? Are there sinister forces out there, attempting to gain entrance into our lives and hearts through any means possible?

It is an important question—one that deserves careful consideration.

5

Sin and Righteousness

Was the death of Jesus a mere incident in His life?
Was it something that just happened? Did He
become a martyr to a righteous cause? Was His
death a sacrifice of a holy life brought about by
sinful men? Was it a natural climax to a struggle
between good and evil? The New Testament declares that Jesus came to die, that He had known
in advance that He came to die, that His death
was for all mankind, that it was the instrument
of accomplishing His Mission.

Arthur Kac[1]

What exactly is "sin"?
This seems like a simple enough question to an-
swer. Just look at the terrible things going on in the world, murders and muggings and wars. Surely all of these things are sins.

And yet, some people will tell you that sin does not really
exist—that it is just an archaic term that no longer applies

to life in the 21st century. We are living in the age of "If it feels good, do it" and "If you believe it is right for you, it must be true." Most people think it is okay to cheat to get ahead. After all, everyone does it.

No wonder the world has become such a dangerous, uncertain place. Do you know what schoolteachers of fifty years ago listed as their number one problem? Students chewing gum in class. Do you know what it is today? Students assaulting teachers. My, how things have changed.

On second thought, perhaps the world was a better place when we all believed in sin.

Sin is real. It is pervasive. Left unchecked, it is as deadly as any cancer. But sin is not so easy to see.

Defining Sin

Maybe it will help us nail down a meaning for this thing called sin if we take a look at the definitions in the Merriam-Webster dictionary:

a. An offense against religious or moral law

b. An action that is or is thought to be highly reprehensible

c. A transgression of the law of God

These definitions are not very specific. Whose religious or moral laws? Whose God? After all, there are many cultures and many religions. What might be a sin in one culture might be completely acceptable in another. Is there a universal or all-inclusive definition of sin? Who by right should be the judge of what is or is not a sin? And has sin always been a part of our world?

To answer those questions, we need to go back to sin's origin. Back to the very beginning, when it first reared its ugly head. Back to the Garden of Eden.

The book of Genesis tells us that God created Adam and Eve in His "image and likeness." What is the difference between these two words? *Image* describes Adam and Eve's potential to be like God their Creator; *likeness* is that potential realized. To help Adam and Eve reach that potential, God gave them "freedom," or what we commonly call "free will." That is what got us into trouble.

God told Adam and Eve not to eat the fruit of the Tree of Knowledge of Good and Evil, but He did not take away their ability to do so. You, no doubt, know what happened next. Eve was tempted by Satan (the serpent), ate of the fruit and then shared it with Adam. Having followed their own wills and ignored God's, they brought sin into the world.

In their act of disobedience, they used their free will to gratify their own individuality rather than to show love and deference to God. And by elevating "self" over God's image, they allowed sin to enter the world for the first time, causing alienation not only between man and God but between man and other men, man and nature, even between man and himself. Death, the result of man's alienation against himself, thus entered the world.

I believe that sin is anything that separates us from God. It is interesting to note that in the New Testament, the term *sin* comes from a Greek word in the field of archery meaning "missing the mark or target." So what is this "target" our lives should be aiming for and yet miss? The target is Yeshua. And our redemption (righteousness) will be healing and transfiguration through His grace.

In Romans 3:23 we are told that "all have sinned and fall short of the glory of God," so we have all "missed the mark." What can we do in this hopeless situation? Fortunately for us, God has promised to "fix things." Right after the Fall in the Garden of Eden, we are promised a Redeemer in Genesis 3:14–15:

> ADONAI Elohim said to the serpent, "Because you did this, cursed are you above all the livestock and above every animal of the field. On your belly will you go, and dust will you eat all the days of your life. I will put animosity between you and the woman—between your seed and her seed. He will crush your head, and you will crush his heel."

This Scripture is actually considered a foreshadowing of the Gospel, called the "protoevangelium." God, in His mercy, intends to help mankind get back to a right relationship with Him by sending us His Son, Yeshua, the Messiah. Years mean nothing to God, who created time and is not bound by it; but from a human viewpoint, it took a long time, centuries, before the Redeemer/Messiah was to arrive on the scene. Through Noah's son Shem a great lineage arose, the line of Abraham, from whom would come the nation of Israel (see Genesis 11:10–26; 12:1–3) and, "in the fullness of time," the Messiah (see Galatians 4:4–5). The Messiah would triumph over sin in a most unexpected way, by giving His blood and body as an atoning sacrifice.

Forgiven, One Year at a Time

God appointed the nation of Israel to be His chosen people—the nation through whom the Messiah would come—

establishing various covenants with them and giving them His laws at Mount Sinai after the exodus from Egypt.

Did the Israelites keep God's laws? Not at all! Time and again they broke His commandments, thus perpetuating the sin that Adam and Eve had brought into the world.

In His wisdom, God established an appointed day, the Day of Atonement, during which the Israelites could be forgiven of their sins. The Bible tells us that there is no forgiveness without the shedding of blood (Hebrews 9:22), and this has been true from the very beginning of time. Leviticus 17:11 says, "For the life of the creature is in the blood, and I have given it to you on the altar to make atonement for your lives—for it is the blood that makes atonement because of the life."

Again, a blood sacrifice is required for the forgiveness of sins. (You may remember that Cain killed his brother, Abel, in a jealous rage because Abel's sacrifice was accepted by God while his was not. That is because Abel offered up the firstborn of his flock—a sacrifice of blood—while Cain offered some vegetables he had harvested.) Bulls, sheep and goats were therefore sacrificed on the altar on the Day of Atonement.

It would be incorrect to say, however, that the sins of the Israelites were forgiven on this day. Instead, their guilt was pushed forward until the next Day of Atonement, when the sacrifices would be offered up again, bringing another year of forgiveness. In other words, if the Israelites did as God commanded and offered sacrifices each year on the Day of Atonement, they would get a one-year reprieve until the next Day of Atonement. The sacrifices the people made were a temporary measure, a foreshadowing of what was to come when the Messiah gave Himself as a sacrifice to forgive their sins—and the sins of all who trust in Him—forever!

The book of Hebrews puts it like this:

The Torah has a shadow of the good things to come—not the form itself of the realities. For this reason it can never, by means of the same sacrifices they offer constantly year after year, make perfect those who draw near. Otherwise, would they not have ceased to be offered, since the worshipers—cleansed once and for all—would no longer have consciousness of sins? But in these sacrifices is a reminder of sins year after year—for it is impossible for the blood of bulls and goats to take away sins. So when Messiah comes into the world, He says, "Sacrifice and offering You did not desire, but a body You prepared for Me. In whole burnt offerings and sin offerings You did not delight. Then I said, 'Behold, I come to do Your will, O God (in the scroll of the book it is written of Me).'" After saying above, "Sacrifices and offerings and whole burnt offerings and sin offerings You did not desire, nor did You delight in them" (those which are offered according to Torah), then He said, "Behold, I come to do Your will." He takes away the first to establish the second. By His will we have been made holy through the offering of the body of Messiah Yeshua once for all.

Hebrews 10:1–10

Power in the Blood

Years ago, I came across a powerful book called *Eternity in Their Hearts*, written by a missionary named Don Richardson. The title is taken from Ecclesiastes 3:11, "He has set eternity in their heart."

In his book, Richardson showed that many of the world's cultures seem to have some knowledge of God and His laws, even though they have never read the Bible, been visited by missionaries or had contact with Christians or Jews. They have an innate awareness that there is a God who made the heavens and the earth, and they believe that He is calling out to them.

This knowledge may have come through supernatural revelation. Or it may have been passed down through hundreds of generations, held on to but distorted due to the passage of time. Perhaps it is true that as humankind spread out across the earth in the early days of civilization, their beliefs changed. They forgot about the old God—but not entirely. They began to worship idols, animals, volcanoes, the sun, what have you, but many of their customs and legends retained some elements of the truth they had once known.

One such belief is that there is a special power in blood to bring about forgiveness and unity.

In 1885, a man by the name of H. Clay Trumbull wrote another fascinating book titled *The Blood Covenant*. The book has been published many times since and continues to be regarded as an important theological work.

As a blurb on the back of the book explains,

The blood covenant is the most solemn, binding agreement possible between two parties. Perhaps one of the least understood, and yet most important and relevant factors in the covenant relationships that God has chosen to employ in His dealings with man, is the blood covenant. This covenant of life and death spans the entire sacrificial system of the Old Testament, and it is the basis for the act of Communion in the Church today. "The author seems to prove beyond a doubt that the blood covenant is one of the most ancient and universal institutions. This idea is founded on

67

the representation familiar to Old Testament scholars, that the blood stands for life."[2]

When you were a child, did you have a blood brother or blood sister? It worked like this: You pricked your finger, causing it to bleed a little, and your friend did the same. Then you pressed your finger to his, or hers, so that you mixed a bit of your blood. (At least you tried.) That gave you and your friend a special bond that neither one of you could break. (Do you know where your blood brother is today?)

You probably did not know it, but you were taking part in one of the world's oldest and most solemn rituals—a ritual that reflects the Torah's teaching on the sacredness of blood.

Trumbull writes that the "primitive rite" of blood covenanting deserves much more attention than it gets, that "there are traces of it, from time immemorial, in every quarter of the globe; yet it has been strangely overlooked by biblical critics and biblical commentators generally, in these later centuries."[3]

Trumbull gives numerous instances from cultures all around the world where this blood covenant rite is carried out. It has been practiced in Europe, Africa, China and among the natives of North and South America. References to the ritual have even been found in a coffin dating to Egypt's Eleventh Dynasty, before the time of Abraham.

Five centuries before Yeshua's birth, Greek historian Herodotus wrote,

> Now the Scythians make covenants in the following manner, with whosoever they make them. Having poured out wine into a great earthen drinking bowl, they mingle with it the blood of those cutting covenant, striking the body [of each

person having a part in it] with a small knife, or cutting it slightly with a sword. Thereafter, they dip into the bowl sword, arrows, axe, and javelin. But while they are doing this they utter many invokings [of curse upon a breach of this covenant]; and, afterwards, not only those who make the covenant, but those of their followers who are of the highest rank, drink off [the wine mingled with blood].[4]

Trumbull also offers these examples of covenant-making:

In Brazil, the Indians were said to have a rite of brotherhood so close and sacred that, as in the case of the Bed'ween beyond the Jordan, its covenanting parties were counted as of one blood; so that marriage between those thus linked would be deemed incestuous. . . .

A similar tie of adopted brotherhood, or of close and sacred friendship, is recognized among the North American Indians. Writing of the Dakota, or the Sioux, Dr. Riggs, the veteran missionary and scholar, says: "Where one Dakota takes another as his *koda* . . . they become brothers in each other's families and are, as such, of course, unable to intermarry."[5]

As the great missionary David Livingstone made his way through Africa, he was asked again and again to make a blood covenant with the chiefs and other leaders of various tribes. Once this was done, the people welcomed him as a brother and were anxious to hear what he had to say about God.

Trumbull tells of two young men who entered into a blood covenant in a village of Lebanon:

Their relatives and neighbors were called together, in the open place before the village fountain, to witness the sealing compact. The young men publicly announced their purpose, and their reasons for it. Their declarations were written down, in

duplicate—one paper for each friend—and signed by themselves and several witnesses. One of the friends took a sharp
lancet, and opened a vein in the other's arm. Into the opening
thus made, he inserted a quill, through which he sucked the
living blood. The lancet-blade was carefully wiped on one
of the duplicate covenant papers, and then it was taken by
the other friend, who made a like incision in its first user's
arm, and drank his blood through the quill, wiping the blade
on the duplicate covenant-record. The two friends declared
together: "We are brothers in a covenant made before God.
Who deceiveth the other, him will God deceive."[6]

Unbreakable!

The blood covenant cannot be broken. Trumbull writes,

As it is the inter-commingling of very lives, nothing can tran-
scend it. It forms a tie, or a union, which cannot be dissolved.
In marriage, divorce is a possibility; not so in the covenant
of blood. . . . The root idea of this rite of blood-friendship
seems to include the belief that the blood is the life of a living being; not merely that the blood is essential to life, but
that, in a peculiar sense, it is life; that it actually vivifies by
its presence; and that by its passing from one organism to
another it carries and imparts life. The inter-commingling
of the blood of two organisms is, therefore, according to
this view, equivalent to the inter-commingling of the lives of
the personalities of the natures, thus brought together; so
that there is, thereby and thenceforward one life in the two
bodies, a common life between the two friends.[7]

This is also true of the covenant God has made with His
people. He has, in essence, given His blood to us, through His

sacrificial death on the cross—through the piercing of His hands and feet and the spear cast into His side, the wound from which blood and water poured forth. If you belong to Yeshua, you are His blood brother or blood sister, and nothing can break that bond!

It is certainly a curious thing to find this blood covenant ritual widely practiced in cultures that otherwise have almost nothing in common. How did it reach from ancient Egypt to China to the isolated tribes of the African interior to the Dakota people of North America?

Did this ritual spring from the blood covenant that was established between God and His people in the early days of creation—after humankind fell from grace in the Garden of Eden?

We have already seen that Abel pleased God by offering a blood sacrifice. After Abel was killed by his jealous brother, God told Cain that "the voice of your brother's blood is crying out to Me from the ground" (Genesis 4:10). Move ahead to Genesis 8, after the cataclysmic flood that destroyed all life on earth except for Noah, his family and the animals they had with them on the ark. After the waters subsided and Noah and his family were able to come out of the ark, the first thing he did was offer a blood sacrifice:

> Noah came out, with his sons, his wife, and his sons' wives. Every animal—every crawling creature, every flying creature, everything that crawls upon the land—came out from the ark in their families. Then Noah built an altar to ADONAI and he took of every clean domestic animal and of every clean flying creature and he offered burnt offerings on the altar. When ADONAI smelled the soothing aroma, ADONAI said in His heart, "I will never again curse the ground on

71

account of man, even though the inclination of the heart of humankind is evil from youth. Nor will I ever again smite all living creatures, as I have done."

Genesis 8:18–21

God was pleased with Noah's sacrifice and went on to give him a new commandment that had to do with the sanctity of blood:

Every crawling thing that is alive will be food for you, as are the green plants—I have now given you everything. Only flesh with its life—that is, its blood—you must not eat! Surely your lifeblood will I avenge. From every animal and from every person will I avenge it. From every person's brother will I avenge that person's life. The one who sheds human blood, by a human will his blood be shed, for in God's image He made humanity.

Genesis 9:3–6

Trumbull points out that this command is reiterated in the book of Acts. When the apostles met in Jerusalem to compose a letter to Gentile believers, they wrote,

It seemed good to the Ruach ha-Kodesh and to us not to place on you any greater burden than these essentials: that you abstain from things offered to idols, from blood, from things strangled, and from sexual immorality. By keeping away from these things, you will do well. Shalom!

Acts 15:28–29

Again, a blood covenant was established with Abraham, the patriarch of the Jewish people—and, in fact, all people of faith. This was done when Abraham showed that he was

72

willing to give his son, Isaac, as a burnt sacrifice and, again, when Abraham gave his own blood through the ritual of circumcision (see Genesis 17:11). We also see this very clearly in Genesis 15:9–21, where we are told, "ADONAI cut a covenant with Abram" (verse 18).

The blood covenant between God and His people was reaffirmed on the first Passover, when God was about to bring the Israelites out of slavery in Egypt. He told them to choose a lamb without blemish, a male of the first year, and put the blood of that lamb on the doorposts and crossbeams of their houses. God says, "The blood will be a sign for you on the houses where you are. When I see the blood, I will pass over you. So there will be no plague among you to destroy you when I strike the land of Egypt" (Exodus 12:13). The blood on the doorposts is a reminder of the blood covenant that exists between God and the descendants of Abraham. The choice of a lamb without blemish looked forward to the day when Yeshua would shed His blood on Calvary to protect us all from the wrath of God, which we deserve because of our sins.

Trumbull also writes that the blood covenant was again reaffirmed at Mount Sinai, on the way to the Promised Land after the Israelites had left Egypt.

So Moses wrote down all the words of ADONAI, then rose up early in the morning, and built an altar below the mountain, along with twelve pillars for the twelve tribes of Israel. He then sent out young men of Bnei-Yisrael, who sacrificed burnt offerings and fellowship offerings of oxen to ADONAI. Then Moses took half of the blood and put it in basins and the other half he poured out against the altar. He took the Scroll of the Covenant and read it in the hearing of the people. Again they said, "All that ADONAI has spoken, we will do and obey." Then Moses took the blood, sprinkled it on the people, and said, "Behold the blood of the covenant, which ADONAI has cut with you, in agreement with all these words."

Exodus 24:4–8

Then, "in the fullness of time, there came down into this world He who from the beginning was one with God, and who now became one with man." Yeshua came, Turnbull writes, "to meet and to satisfy the holiest and uttermost yearnings of the human soul after eternal life, in communion and union with God."[8]

Yeshua Is the Living Bread

The meaning of the blood covenant is fulfilled in the death and resurrection of Yeshua, who says,

> I am the living bread, which came down from heaven. If anyone eats this bread, he will live forever. This bread is My flesh, which I will give for the life of the world . . . unless you eat the flesh of the Son of Man and drink His blood, you have no life in yourselves. He who eats My flesh and drinks My blood has eternal life, and I will raise him up on the last day. For My flesh is real food and My blood is real drink. He who eats My flesh and drinks My blood abides in Me, and I in him.
>
> John 6:51, 53–56

Paul reiterated this in his letter to the believers at Corinth:

> For I received from the Lord what I also passed on to you— that the Lord Yeshua, on the night He was betrayed, took

matzah; and when He had given thanks, He broke it and said, "This is My body, which is for you. Do this in memory of Me." In the same way, He also took the cup, after supper, saying, "This cup is the new covenant in My blood. Do this, as often as you drink it, in memory of Me."

1 Corinthians 11:23–25

Clay Trumbull gracefully depicted the fulfillment of the blood covenant when he wrote,

Here was the communion feast, in partaking of the flesh of the fitting and accepted sacrifice; toward which all rite and symbol, and all heart yearning and inspired prophecy had pointed, in all the ages. Here was the realization of promise and hope and longing, in man's possibility of inter-union with God through a common life—which is oneness of blood; and in man's inter-communion with God, through participation in the blessings of a common table. He who could speak for God here proffered of his own blood, to make those whom he loved of the same nature with himself, and so of the same nature with his God; to bring them into blood-friendship with their God; and he proffered of his own body, to supply them with soul nourishment, in that Bread which came down from God.[9]

Yeshua went to the cross for your sin . . . and mine. Isaiah 53, known as the suffering servant passage, makes this abundantly clear:

Who has believed our report? To whom is the arm of ADONAI revealed? For He grew up before Him like a tender shoot, like a root out of dry ground. He had no form or majesty that we should look at Him, nor beauty that we should desire Him. He was despised and rejected by men, a man of

75

sorrows, acquainted with grief, One from whom people hide their faces. He was despised, and we did not esteem Him. Surely He has borne our griefs and carried our pains. Yet we esteemed Him stricken, struck by God, and afflicted. But He was pierced because of our transgressions, crushed because of our iniquities. The chastisement for our shalom was upon Him, and by His stripes we are healed.

We all like sheep have gone astray. Each of us turned to his own way. So ADONAI has laid on Him the iniquity of us all. He was oppressed and He was afflicted yet He did not open His mouth. Like a lamb led to the slaughter, like a sheep before its shearers is silent, so He did not open His mouth. Because of oppression and judgment He was taken away. As for His generation, who considered? For He was cut off from the land of the living, for the transgression of my people—the stroke was theirs. His grave was given with the wicked, and by a rich man in His death, though He had done no violence, nor was there any deceit in His mouth.

Yet it pleased ADONAI to bruise Him. He caused Him to suffer. If He makes His soul a guilt offering, He will see His offspring, He will prolong His days, and the will of ADONAI will succeed by His hand. As a result of the anguish of His soul He will see it and be satisfied by His knowledge. The Righteous One, My Servant will make many righteous and He will bear their iniquities. Therefore I will give Him a portion with the great, and He will divide the spoil with the mighty—because He poured out His soul to death, and was counted with transgressors. For He bore the sin of many, and interceded for the transgressors.

This is a long passage but well worth noting, as it clearly foreshadows Yeshua and His blood sacrifice to atone for all of mankind's transgressions.

I cannot help but look upon it as a prayer reminding me of what Yeshua, in His mercy and love, did for me and all mankind.

No Further Need for Sacrifice

The Torah clearly teaches that a blood sacrifice is necessary for the forgiveness of sins, but no sacrifices are offered in Judaism today. When the Temple was destroyed by the Romans in AD 70, blood sacrifices were effectively ended. I believe that one of the reasons for this was that such sacrifices were no longer necessary after Yeshua shed His blood for all mankind, Jews and Gentiles alike.

Yeshua talks about the New Covenant of His blood at His final Passover with His disciples, often referred to as the Last Supper. It is this "blood sacrifice" that He offers, both in the cup of wine as the "cup of redemption" and at Golgotha, that is given for the once-and-for-all redemption of humankind. And it is Yeshua's crucifixion on the cross that finally removes the stain of Adam and Eve's sin of disobedience in the Garden of Eden.

So it is Yeshua who is the fulfillment of God's promise in Genesis, and it is through Him that we have received atonement, forgiveness and redemption.

Proof in the Resurrection

Is there proof that Yeshua is exactly who He claimed to be—and that we can obtain righteousness by accepting His sacrifice on our behalf?

In a word, yes.

There is proof in the millions of lives that have been changed by faith in Him. People have been set free from afflictions, addictions and difficulties of all kinds. They have been delivered from debilitating fear and face the future with hope. And there is proof because Jesus walked out of the tomb, alive again after being executed by crucifixion.

But is there evidence that the resurrection really happened? The answer is a resounding yes.

First of all, the resurrection did not happen "a long time ago in a galaxy far far away." It happened at a specific place and time—Jerusalem during Passover—around AD 30. Because it is so specific, it should have been fairly easy to disprove if it were not true. And yet, even those who lived in Jerusalem at the time and hated Yeshua so much they killed Him were not able to disprove it.

As I said in my book *A Rabbi Looks at Jesus of Nazareth*,

> Suppose I write a book about Elvis Presley in which I claim that he had been raised from the dead. Do you think anyone would believe me (outside of a few people who get their information from *The National Enquirer*)? Of course not. Even though Presley has been dead for decades, many people remember him and know that he did not come back from the grave. Similarly, when the New Testament was written, many people who had been alive during the time of Yeshua lived and was crucified were still in Israel. If they knew that He had never come out of that tomb they would have said so, and the newly birthed movement of His followers would have crumbled.
>
> Now, I am not trying for a minute to equate Jesus of Nazareth with Elvis Presley, except to show that you cannot get away with making up wild stories about people—even if they have been gone for thirty years or more. In the first few decades

after Yeshua's resurrection, no one ever tried to claim that the story was pure fiction. Even the Jewish leaders who were opposed to Him admitted that *something* strange had happened. So instead of denying the entire story, they accused His disciples of stealing His body.

What they did not acknowledge was that this would have been impossible, since guards were posted at the tomb to make sure this did not happen. Besides, the tomb was sealed with a stone that could not be moved without the combined effort of several strong men. Nobody could have sneaked into the cemetery, snatched the body and made a quick getaway.[10]

Theologian, author and expert on the resurrection William Lane Craig agrees that both believers in Yeshua and Jews who opposed Him were convinced that the tomb was empty.

The site of Jesus' tomb was known to Christian and Jew alike. So if it weren't empty, it would be impossible for a movement founded on belief in the Resurrection to have come into existence in the same city where this man had been publicly executed and buried. . . . The earliest Jewish polemic presupposes the historicity of the empty tomb. In other words, there was nobody who was claiming that the tomb still contained Jesus' body. The question always was, "What happened to the body?" The Jews proposed the ridiculous story that the guards had fallen asleep. Obviously, they were grasping at straws. But the point is this: they started with the assumption that the tomb was vacant! Why? Because they knew it was![11]

Case in point: Justin Martyr's *Dialogue with Trypho*, written around AD 150, is the record of a conversation between Justin, a believer in Yeshua, and Trypho, a Jewish nonbeliever. At one point, Trypho makes this claim about Yeshua:

79

[He was] a Galilean deceiver, whom we crucified; but his disciples stole him by night from the tomb, where he was laid when unfastened from the cross, and now deceive men by asserting that he has risen from the dead and ascended into heaven.[12]

The most amazing thing about stories like this is that they openly admit that Jesus' body was missing from the tomb. As John R. W. Stott writes, the theory that the apostles stole Jesus' body "is so unlikely as to be virtually impossible. If anything is clear from the Gospels and the Acts, it is that the apostles were sincere. . . . Hypocrites and martyrs are not made of the same stuff."[13]

And though there is no eyewitness account of the moment that Yeshua's body came back to life after having been crucified, author and philosopher Gary Habermas argues that an eyewitness is not necessary for belief in the resurrection: "Here's how I look at the evidence for the Resurrection: First, did Jesus die on the cross? And second, did he appear later to people? If you can establish those two things, you've made your case, because dead people don't normally do that."[14]

Habermas is exactly right. On the second point—did people see Yeshua alive after He died?—we have testimony that He appeared to many people, who recognized that He was alive and well, after His crucifixion. Some walked with Him on the road to Emmaus. Others ate a meal with Him on the shore of the Sea of Galilee. His apostles watched as He ascended into heaven.

The apostle Paul writes of literally hundreds of people who saw Yeshua alive after the cross:

He appeared to Cephas, and then to the Twelve. After that, he appeared to more than five hundred of the brothers and sisters at the same time, most of whom are still living, though some have fallen asleep. Then he appeared to James, then to all the apostles, and last of all he appeared to me also, as to one abnormally born.

1 Corinthians 15:5–8 NIV

Note that Paul said most of these people were still living when he wrote this, and they could have been questioned. While it is easy to doubt a handful of people claiming to have seen a dead person resurrected, it is almost impossible to refute the testimony of hundreds who saw Yeshua on different occasions after His death.

Other Evidence for the Resurrection

What about Habermas's first point? Did Jesus really die on the cross? The apostle John writes of the crucifixion:

It was the Day of Preparation, and the next day was a festival Shabbat. So that the bodies should not remain on the execu tion stake during Shabbat, the Judean leaders asked Pilate to have the legs broken and to have the bodies taken away. So the soldiers came and broke the legs of the first and then the other who had been executed with Yeshua. Now when they came to Yeshua and saw that He was already dead, they did not break His legs. But one of the soldiers pierced His side with a spear, and immediately blood and water came out. He who has seen it has testified, and his testimony is true. He knows that he is telling the truth, so that you also may believe.

John 19:31–35

According to experts like Dr. Alexander Metherell, this passage proves Jesus died of heart failure:

Even before he died, the hypovolemic shock would have caused a sustained rapid heart rate that would have contributed to heart failure, resulting in the collection of fluid in the membrane around the heart, called a pericardial effusion, as well as around the lungs, which is called a pleural effusion.[15]

This shows that the spear thrust into Jesus' side passed through a lung and into his heart. When it was withdrawn, the doctor explains, this clear, watery fluid would have flowed out of the wound, followed by "a large volume of blood."[16] Metherell says that "the spear thrust into his heart would have settled the issue once and for all. And the Romans weren't about to risk their own deaths by allowing him to walk away alive."[17]

Drs. Brad Harrub and Bert Thompson agree with Metherell's assessment:

Much speculation has centered on the exact location of the puncture wound and thus the source of the resulting blood and water. However, the Greek word (*pleura*) that John used clearly denotes the area of the intercoastal [*sic*] ribs that cover the lungs. Given the upward angle of the spear, and the thoracic location of the wound, abdominal organs can be ruled out as having provided the blood and water. A more likely scenario would suggest that the piercing affected a lung (along with any built-up fluid), the pericardial sac surrounding the heart, the right atrium of the heart itself, the pulmonary vessels, and/or the aorta. Since John did not describe the specific side of the body on which the wound was inflicted, we can only speculate about which structures might have been impaled by such a vicious act. However, the blood could have resulted from the heart, the aorta, or any of the pulmonary vessels. Water probably was provided by pleural or pericardial fluids (that surround the lungs and heart).[18]

In his book *Evidence That Demands a Verdict*, Josh McDowell quotes Bishop E. LeCamus of La Rochelle, France, as saying that even if Jesus had been alive when He was taken from the cross, He would have died in the tomb, "as the contact of the body with the cold stone of the sepulcher would have been enough to bring on a syncope through the congelation of the blood, owing to the fact that the regular circulation was already checked."[19] He goes on to say that a man who has fainted is not revived by being shut up in a cave, but rather by being exposed to open air.

Based on our modern medical knowledge—which is clearly compatible with the observations of Yeshua's crucifixion recorded in the gospels—we have no reason to doubt the biblical account that Jesus did in fact die as a result of the trauma of being crucified.

It Is All about Yeshua

All through the Word of God, the prevailing theme is that our salvation and restoration to a proper relationship with God can only be achieved through acceptance of His Son, Yeshua, as our Redeemer and Savior. Jews and Gentiles must be united in acknowledgment of Yeshua as mankind's Redeemer and Savior in order for God the Creator's promise of redemption and righteousness to prevail.

But now God's righteousness apart from the Torah has been revealed, to which the Torah and the Prophets bear witness— namely, the righteousness of God through putting trust in

83

Messiah Yeshua, to all who keep on trusting. For there is no distinction, for all have sinned and fall short of the glory of God. They are set right as a gift of His grace, through the redemption that is in Messiah Yeshua. God set forth Yeshua as an atonement, through faith in His blood, to show His righteousness in passing over sins already committed. Through God's forbearance, He demonstrates His righteousness at the present time—that He Himself is just and also the justifier of the one who puts his trust in Yeshua. Where, then, is boasting? It is excluded. By what principle? Of works? No, but by the principle of faith. For we consider a person to be set right apart from Torah observance. Is God the God of the Jewish people only? Is He not also the God of the Gentiles? Yes, of the Gentiles also. Since God is One, He will set right the circumcised by faith and the uncircumcised through faith. Do we then nullify the Torah through faithfulness? May it never be! On the contrary, we uphold the Torah.

Romans 3:21–31

Yeshua confirmed this. "Then they said to Him, 'What shall we do to perform the works of God?' Yeshua answered them, 'This is the work of God, to trust in the One He sent'" (John 6:28–29).

Sin entered the world when Adam and Eve ate of the fruit from the Tree of Knowledge of Good and Evil. This brought about man's alienation from God the Creator and even from himself, thus bringing death into the world and banishing man from the Garden of Eden. But not for eternity.

God promised to send a Savior and Redeemer to wipe away man's guilt and sins and restore him to a personal relationship with his Creator. Yeshua, as promised in the Scriptures of the Old Testament, kept God the Creator's promise, making

84

of Himself a blood sacrifice in our stead and proving by His resurrection that we are now restored to His righteousness.

Our road to peace with God requires only one action on our part—that we accept Yeshua as our Redeemer and Lord. When we do this sincerely, life returns as God intended, and we are empowered by His Spirit to spread His Word and do the good works He has instructed us to do. Yeshua Himself gives us these comforting words:

> Do not let your heart be troubled. Trust in God; trust also in Me. In My Father's house there are many dwelling places. If it were not so, would I have told you that I am going to prepare a place for you? If I go and prepare a place for you, I will come again and take you to Myself, so that where I am you may also be.
>
> John 14:1–3

Heaven in all its glory. Eternal communion with our Creator and His only Son. No more sin. Only true righteousness for all eternity. The very thought fills me with awe and gratitude.

6

The Problem of Evil

For our struggle is not against flesh and blood,
but against the rulers, against the powers, against
the worldly forces of this darkness, and against
the spiritual forces of wickedness in the heavenly
places. Therefore, take up the full armor of God,
so that you may be able to resist when the times
are evil, and after you have done everything, to
stand firm.

Ephesians 6:12–13

Sarah is just seven years old, and she has seen more pain and loss than most people will see in a lifetime.

She lives with her mother in a crowded refugee camp in Uganda, Africa, without adequate food, water, shelter, clothing or health care. She sleeps on a hard dirt floor, shivering in the cold, without a blanket to cover her.

Six months ago, she lived with her parents and two older brothers in a peaceful village in South Sudan. Sarah's family was not rich by any means, but her mother and father grew enough food on their land to keep Sarah and her siblings fed. Sarah was just starting to attend the local school, and she loved learning with her friends. Most of all, she felt loved and secure. She knew nothing at all about things like politics or war. Nor did she know how cruel people could be to one another.

Everything changed one afternoon when the sound of automatic gunfire echoed through her village. People began screaming, crying and running for their lives as the gunfire grew louder—and closer.

Sarah put her hands over her ears and began to cry as her father and mother burst into the house. They looked terrified.

Her mother grabbed her hand and pulled her toward the door.

"Come on!" she shouted. "We have to run!"

Outside, many of Sarah's neighbors and friends were running into the bush. Behind them, Sarah saw men pointing rifles at the fleeing villagers. More gunshots sounded; some screamed and fell to the ground!

Other men dressed in military uniforms were using torches to set the thatched roofs of huts on fire. Her mother urged her forward just as she saw her own home being set ablaze.

Sarah does not remember for certain what happened next.

She saw her brother stumble and fall and her father turn around to help him. She wanted to stop, too, but her mother yanked her forward. She has not seen her father or brother since that day.

She and her mother kept on running, deeper into the bush, headed for the safety of the Uganda border. Their journey continued for almost a week. Often they hid in the bush during the day and traveled at night to avoid being captured. They had almost nothing to eat. The African sun beat down until their throats were dry and they feared they would die of thirst.

Somehow, they made it into Uganda, which was taking in hundreds of thousands of refugees from both South Sudan and the Democratic Republic of the Congo.

Sarah is safe from bombs and bullets—at least for now. But what will tomorrow bring? Will she and her mother ever be able to rebuild their lives? Will Sarah be able to go back to school and get the education she needs to build a better life? And what has become of her father and brother? Are they alive somewhere, or were they murdered by the soldiers who attacked her village?

Tragically, Sarah's story is not unique.

She is one of many thousands of children all over the world who are suffering terribly—when they should be cherished and loved, running, laughing, playing games with their friends and enjoying the carefree days of childhood.

Evil is alive and well on planet earth.

What Happened to Harmony and Understanding?

Way back in 1968, a group called The 5th Dimension recorded a version of the song "Age of Aquarius." Written for the musical *Hair*, it looked ahead to the dawning of a new age when peace, love and harmony abounded—a hippie utopia brought about by uniting the world against war and abandoning the traditional mores of the characters' parents. The song was a huge hit, topping the charts for six weeks in 1969 and winning The 5th Dimension two Grammys in 1970. Apparently it resonated with people all over the United States and Canada.

So, how has the world been over the past 48 years? Have we eradicated evil and built a world where, in the words of the song, "sympathy and trust abound"?

Not exactly.

A quick look at just about any TV news program will tell you that in our world hatred and violence abound. Just think about how many mass shootings we have seen in the United States over the past few years.

- April 16, 2007: Seung-Hui Cho, a student at Virginia Tech University, opens fire on campus, killing 32 people.

- November 5, 2009: Major Nidal Malik Hasan, an Army psychiatrist, kills 13 people and wounds 32 others in a shooting at Fort Hood, Texas.

- July 20, 2012: James Holmes, 24, opens fire in a movie theater in Aurora, Colorado, during a showing of the Batman movie *The Dark Knight Rises*. Twelve people are killed and 70 injured.

- December 14, 2012: Adam Lanza, 20, forces his way into Sandy Hook Elementary School in Newtown, Connecticut, and kills 26 people, including 20 first-graders.

- June 17, 2015: Dylann Roof murders 9 in a shooting attack at a historic black church in Charleston, South Carolina.

- December 2, 2015: A married couple shoots up a company Christmas gathering in San Bernardino, California, killing 14 people and wounding 22. Syed

90

Rizwan Farook and his wife, Tashfeen Malik, were killed in a gun battle with police.

- June 12, 2016: Gunman Omar Mateen attacks a gay nightclub in Orlando, Florida, killing 49 and wounding 53. Mateen swore allegiance to ISIS in the worst terrorist attack in America since 9/11.

This is by no means an exhaustive list. It is but a sampling of the evil that is being unleashed on a regular basis here in America and around the world.

Darkness Abounds

Consider what is happening in Iraq and Syria, where Islamic State terrorists are brutalizing and killing thousands of innocent civilians. Men, women and children are being beaten, beheaded and even crucified—many of them for refusing to renounce their faith in Yeshua. My morning newspaper recently reported that extremists in Mali shot and killed 28 people at a hotel, and these kinds of violent acts are so common these days that it did not even make the front page. As I am writing this, the last half year has seen 130 people killed in coordinated terrorist attacks in the streets of Paris, 14 people slaughtered in San Bernardino and 31 killed in explosions detonated by terrorists in Brussels, Belgium. And the worst terrorist attack since 9/11 just took place in Orlando, where more than 100 Americans were killed or injured.

We cannot blame all of our woes on terrorists, or we would ignore the unimaginable violence of the drug cartels in Mexico, the drive-by killings carried out by teen gangs here in the United States and the never-ending war between Arabs and

Jews in the Middle East, along with thousands of murders, assaults and other violent crimes that take place every day.

I could go on for pages listing the evils that plague our planet—but it would be much too depressing, and I would be covering ground that most of us know all too well from personal experience and through the daily reminders brought our way from newspapers, the Internet and news programs on television and radio.

There was a time when many people believed that the human race was getting better and better. We were no longer barbarians; we were civilized. We looked back on the atrocities that were committed by people in the ancient past and thought, *Thank God we're not like that anymore.*

Then, as the twentieth century ground toward becoming the bloodiest century in history, it proved that humans are just as evil as ever. Two major wars killed an estimated hundred million people, and dozens of smaller conflicts killed and wounded millions more. And the twentieth century produced more than its share of monsters: Adolf Hitler murdered more than six million innocent Jews. Joseph Stalin was responsible for millions of deaths in the Soviet Union. Millions more died at the hands of Mao Tse-tung in China, Pol Pot in Cambodia and Idi Amin in Uganda. The list could go on and on.

And, so far, the 21st century seems well on its way to surpassing the one before.

Where Did Evil Come From?

Why *is* there evil in the world?

This is a very difficult question, but it is one that just about all of us ask at one time or another.

The book of Job, which is considered by many scholars to be the oldest in the Bible, addresses the question of why evil things happen to good people, but it does not give a concise answer. Instead, the point seems to be that suffering and evil are a part of life in this world, and when they come, the only thing we can do is hold on to God and trust that He has it all under control.

In the first few centuries after the second Temple was destroyed by Rome—along with most of Jerusalem—many Jewish rabbis began wrestling with the problem of evil. And no wonder. As many as one million Jews had been slaughtered in the Roman siege of Jerusalem, including women and children. Heaps of bodies were piled in the streets of the holy city, and an estimated hundred thousand Jews were captured and forced into slavery. This was a time of great evil for the Jewish people.

Back in 1981, Rabbi Harold Kushner sought to answer our question about evil in his book *When Bad Things Happen to Good People*. The book, written from the depths of Kushner's grief after the death of his fourteen-year-old son, Aaron, immediately became a runaway bestseller. Over the years, it has sold millions of copies and has been hailed as a classic.

Rabbi Kushner made a lot of good points in his book, especially about how God is with us whenever we go through a difficult time. But his conclusion was, basically, that though God wants to stop our suffering, He cannot, because He is *just not powerful enough*. The rabbi wrote, "I can worship a God who hates suffering but cannot eliminate it, more than I can worship a God who chooses to make children suffer and die, for whatever exalted reason."[1]

My heart goes out to every parent who has watched a child suffer and die. As a father myself, I cannot imagine having to deal with such anguish and grief. But the God I serve does not choose "to make children suffer and die." The God I find in the pages of the Bible, the God I know from personal experience, would never choose to make a child—like Sarah in Uganda—suffer.

He wants the best for everyone. His heart breaks every time one of His children is diagnosed with cancer, suffers from hunger or becomes a victim of terrorist brutality. Which leads us to the important question: If God grieves, why does it happen?

There are two basic answers to this:

1. This world is not the way God intended it to be.
2. We suffer because God has given us free will.

The Bible tells me that the world we live in has been tainted by sin. When God created the first human beings, He intended for them to live forever in paradise. They had everything they could possibly need, including daily fellowship with God Himself. But keeping it all was contingent upon their obedience. Because God had given them free will, they could choose whether or not they would live in obedience, and they chose not to. As a result, sin, death and evil entered the world. In His sovereignty, God has chosen not to violate man's free will. So while God is indeed all-powerful, He has chosen to limit that power.

You may recall that we have talked about Antony Flew, who was once one of the world's leading proponents of atheism. Flew, who came to believe in God, said that he became an atheist at a very young age for two primary reasons. The first was that he felt the problem of evil in the world disproved the existence of an all-good and all-powerful God; the second was that "the 'free-will defense' did not relieve the Creator of responsibility for the manifest ills of creation."[2] Flew later acknowledged that these reasons for embracing atheism were "clearly inadequate."[3]

In addressing these stumbling blocks, C. S. Lewis says,

> Christianity asserts that God is good; that He made all things good and for the sake of their goodness; that one of the good things He made, namely, the free will of rational creatures, by its very nature . . . leaves the way open to a great evil, that of competition and hostility. And if souls are free, they cannot be prevented from dealing with the problem by competition instead of by courtesy. And once they have advanced to actual hostility, they can then exploit the fixed nature of matter to hurt one another. . . . [This] means that when human beings fight the victory ordinarily goes to those who have superior weapons, skill, and numbers, even if their cause is unjust.
>
> We can, perhaps, conceive of a world in which God corrected the results of this abuse of free will by His creatures at every moment: so that a wooden beam became soft as grass when it was used as a weapon, and the air refused to obey me if I attempted to set up in it the soundwaves that carry lies or insults. But such a world would be one in which wrong actions were impossible, and in which, therefore, freedom of the will would be void.[4]

When the first humans disobeyed God's laws, two things happened that changed everything: Sin entered the world and Satan took control of our planet.

Most people tend to think of "sin" as an abstract idea— as something that is not quite "real." But it is much more than that. I believe that sin is a physical and spiritual poison that quickly spread once it entered the world. It was like a burst of chemical warfare, and we still live under its toxic cloud.

Our world has fallen far from what it was supposed to be, and sin's impact is all around us. Sin causes war, crime, disease, terrorism, accidents and natural disasters of all types. It is what causes weeds to grow in your lawn or garden. It is why life in the natural world is often a "kill or be killed" proposition. (Anyone who doubts this is true should watch a few *National Geographic* specials on TV and see how many zebras, gazelles and similar gentle creatures are killed by lions and other predators. Darwin obviously got the idea of survival of the fittest from nature—but he did not take into account how sin corrupted nature.) And sin is why people suffer.

The Bible paints a picture of how the world will be when God has restored it to the way He intended it to be:

> The wolf will dwell with the lamb, the leopard will lie down with the kid, the calf and the young lion and the yearling together, and a little child will lead them. The cow and the bear will graze, their young ones lie down together, and the lion will eat straw like an ox. A nursing child will play by a cobra's hole, and a weaned child will put his hand into a viper's den. They will not hurt or destroy in all My holy mountain, for the earth will be full of the knowledge of ADONAI, as the waters cover the sea.
>
> Isaiah 11:6–9

God intended all of His creatures to live in peace and harmony with one another and with nature. He also intended human beings to rule over creation: "God blessed them and God said to them, 'Be fruitful and multiply, fill the land, and conquer it. Rule over the fish of the sea, the flying creatures of the sky, and over every animal that crawls on the land'" (Genesis 1:28). But after they sinned, He told them,

> Cursed is the ground because of you—with pain will you eat of it all the days of your life. Thorns and thistles will sprout for you. You will eat the plants of the field, by the sweat of your brow will you eat food, until you return to the ground, since from it were you taken. For you are dust, and to dust will you return.
>
> Genesis 3:17–19

When Adam and Eve submitted to Satan, they in essence abdicated the dominion God had given them. They traded their authority to Satan for a few bites of forbidden fruit.

Luke 4 contains an account of how Satan tempted Yeshua after He was baptized.

> And leading Him up, the devil showed Him all the kingdoms of the world in an instant. And the devil said to Him, "I'll give to You all this authority along with its glory, because it has been handed over to me and I can give it to anyone I wish. Therefore, if You will worship before me, all this shall be Yours."
>
> Luke 4:5–7

Yeshua did not give in, but He did not accuse Satan of lying, either. I believe that is because He knew the devil was telling the truth. The authority had been handed over to Satan by Adam and Eve in the Garden of Eden.

97

With Us in Our Pain

I want to go back for just a minute to talk about the one thing I do like about Harold Kushner's book. He is absolutely right when he says that one thing we can always be sure of when times of suffering come our way is that God is right there with us in the midst of our pain. One Bible story that aptly illustrates this is the account of the three young Jewish men, Shadrach, Meshach and Abednego, who were thrown into a fiery furnace by King Nebuchadnezzar. You may remember that the king was outraged because those young men refused to worship the idol he had set up. The king was so angry, in fact, that he had the furnace heated up seven times hotter than normal. Then, he had Shadrach and his friends bound and thrown into the fire. The blaze disintegrated the ropes that bound them, but not a hair on their heads was singed. The king was amazed when he looked into the furnace and saw not three but four men walking around in the flames, completely unscathed, "and the fourth has the appearance like a son of the gods!" (Daniel 3:25).

It was when evil seemed ready to consume them that Shadrach, Meshach and Abednego discovered the power and presence of God. The same thing can and does happen to His people today.

We serve a God that gets right down in the dirt and grime with us. He is not an aloof Being so far above us that He does not care about us.

I love what John R. W. Stott said about this:

> I could never myself believe in God, if it were not for the cross. . . . In the real world of pain, how could one worship a God who was immune to it? I have entered many

Buddhist temples in different Asian countries and stood respectfully before the statue of Buddha, his legs crossed, arms folded, eyes closed, the ghost of a smile playing around his mouth, a remote look on his face, detached from the agonies of the world. But each time after a while I have had to turn away. And in imagination I have turned instead to that lonely, twisted, tortured figure on the cross, nails through hands and feet, back lacerated, limbs wrenched, brow bleeding from thorn-pricks, mouth dry and intolerably thirsty, plunged in God-forsaken darkness. That is the God for me! He laid aside his immunity to pain. He entered our world of flesh and blood, tears and death. He suffered for us. Our sufferings become more manageable in light of his. There is still a question mark against human suffering, but over it we boldly stamp another mark, the cross which symbolizes divine suffering.[5]

Our Attraction to Evil

There is more good news: As much as we hate evil, God hates it more. His heart is broken by the terrible things that happen in this world—things He never wanted to take place. He is distressed by the hold evil has over us.

Not long ago, I had to run into a shopping mall on my way home from the office to pick up a few things. As I walked past a children's clothing store, I was struck by the cute designs I saw—teddy bears, fluffy rabbits, kittens, puppies and all sorts of happy things that bring a smile to the face.

Then I turned a corner and found myself in front of a skate shop for teens. The kittens and puppies had transformed into skulls and crossbones, skeletons, devil's horns and other grotesque, Satanic looking designs. The change that takes place over a few short years is shocking. I could not help but think of how the first human beings came into this world pure and innocent but were corrupted by the cunning and deception of the evil one. I do not think for a minute that this dramatic change is "just one of those things." It happens because there is a battle between good and evil in this world. We all say we hate evil, and yet we are attracted by it. Our enemy, Satan, does everything within his power to get us to join him on the dark side.

The Jewish Talmud tells the story of Eleazar ben Durdaya, who had lived a life of excess and debauchery. He never gave a thought to helping others, or to doing what God wanted him to do, until fairly late in his life.

As old age approached, he began to contemplate his spiritual state. He knew that he had not lived a good life, so he began to blame others for his failures. He blamed the elements, the climate, the environment and other people for all the bad things he had done. He blamed everything and everyone but himself. But when none of those he had accused would accept the blame, he finally had to admit, "The matter then depends on me alone!"

Upon hearing this, Rabbi Judah the Prince, the spiritual leader of that generation, declared, "Some take many years to earn eternal life, but some acquire immortality in one hour!"[6] In other words, when we see the evil of our own hearts, we have made a great breakthrough.

We are all sinners, so we are all in need of a Savior. As the apostle Paul put it, "all have sinned and fall short of the glory of God" (Romans 3:23).

No, things have not changed much at all since the days of Genesis 6:5–6:

Then ADONAI saw that the wickedness of humankind was great on the earth, and that every inclination of the thoughts of their heart was only evil all the time. So ADONAI regretted that He made humankind on the earth, and His heart was deeply pained.

You may remember that God decided to destroy the earth with a great flood, saving only Noah and his family. This fresh start did not last very long. Before much time had passed, human beings were back to their old sinful ways—murdering, robbing, assaulting and otherwise mistreating one another. Such is the pervasiveness of evil.

What about Good in the World?

C. S. Lewis asks an interesting question:

> If the universe is so bad, or even half so bad, how on earth did human beings ever come to attribute it to the activity of a wise and good Creator? . . . Men are fools, perhaps; but hardly so foolish as that.[7]

Philip Yancey said something similar:

> It struck me the other day, after I read my umpteenth book on the problem of pain (the theological question of this century, it seems), that I have never even seen a book on "the problem of pleasure." Nor have I met a philosopher who goes around shaking his head in perplexity over the basic question of why we experience pleasure. A good and loving God would naturally want his creatures to experience delight, joy and personal fulfillment. We Christians start from that assumption and then look for ways to explain the origin of suffering. But don't atheists and secular humanists have an

101

equal obligation to explain the origin of pleasure in a world of randomness and meaninglessness?[8]

As I said when we began, it is not possible to completely resolve here most of the questions we are going to consider in this book. And the question about evil is one of the most difficult. There are no fast and easy answers. But as we near the end of our discussion about evil, I want to tell you about two people who came face-to-face with one of the worst evils the world has ever known. Most of us can never begin to imagine the horrors they endured. And I am not as much interested in talking about why it happened as I am in considering their responses to it.

Their names are Simon Weisenthal and Corrie ten Boom. You have probably heard of both of them.

Simon Weisenthal lost 89 family members to Nazi brutality and came within a few seconds of being shot himself into a trench with 53 other Jews in honor of Adolf Hitler's 54th birthday. The murderers spared his life so he (as an artist) could create a poster in honor of Hitler's birthday instead. After World War II, Wiesenthal spent the rest of his life on the trail of Nazi war criminals, making sure they paid for their crimes.[9] In his book *The Sunflower*, he writes about an event that took place when he was a prisoner in Janowska concentration camp.

One afternoon, Wiesenthal was pulled from his work detail and brought to a badly wounded and dying German officer. He wanted to make a deathbed confession, and Wiesenthal had been chosen to hear it. The man began to talk about his service in Russia and the brutal measures he and his fellow soldiers had taken against the Jews. Once his SS unit had forced a number of them into a building and set it on fire.

Some of the trapped Jews jumped from an upper floor in an attempt to escape the flames. He and the other members of his unit shot them as they fell. Some were children.

For two hours Wiesenthal suffered through the soldier's confession of atrocity after atrocity. Finally the soldier said, "I know that what I am asking is almost too much for you," he said. "But without your answer, I cannot die in peace." Then he begged Wiesenthal to forgive him on behalf of all the Jewish people he had killed, injured and otherwise brutalized.

Wiesenthal stood there for a long moment. How could he forgive a man who had behaved like a monster? How could he be merciful to a man who had shown no mercy to children when they begged him to let them live?

No—he could not do it.

He turned and left the room, leaving the dying soldier alone with his tortured, guilty conscience.

Corrie ten Boom was also imprisoned by the Nazis, not because she was Jewish but because her family was caught hiding Jews to protect them from the Nazis. You may have read her bestselling book, *The Hiding Place*, or seen the movie that starred Julie Harris.

After the war, Corrie traveled widely to preach on the subject of God's forgiveness. One night in Munich, after her talk, she saw a familiar figure coming to shake her hand.

> One moment I saw the overcoat and the brown hat; the next, a blue uniform and a visored cap with its skull and crossbones. . . . Betsie [Corrie's sister] and I had been arrested for concealing Jews in our home during the Nazi occupation of Holland; this man had been a guard at Ravensbrück concentration camp where we were sent.

It was the first time Corrie had come face-to-face with one of her captors. The man admitted his role at Ravensbrück:

> "But since that time," he went on, "I have become a Christian. I know that God has forgiven me for the cruel things I did there, but I would like to hear it from your lips as well. *Fräulein*"—again the hand came out—"will you forgive me?"
>
> I stood there—I whose sins had every day to be forgiven—and could not. Betsie had died in that place—how could he erase her slow, terrible death simply for the asking? . . .
>
> "Jesus, help me!" I prayed silently. "I can lift my hand. I can do that much. You supply the feeling."
>
> And so woodenly, mechanically, I thrust my hand into the one stretched out to me. And as I did, an incredible thing took place. The current started in my shoulder, raced down my arm, sprang into our joined hands. And then this healing warmth seemed to flood my whole being, bringing tears to my eyes.
>
> "I forgive you, brother!" I cried. "With all my heart!"[10]

Now, why was Corrie ten Boom able to forgive?

She did it with the help of the One who had gone to the cross for her, who had taken her sins upon Himself. Because she knew that she had been forgiven of much, she was able to forgive much. I also believe that God gave her the supernatural power she needed to forgive, thus overcoming evil with love.

We have been asking why evil exists, but the only answers I can give are based on speculation. There is no Scripture that tells us for certain how sin and evil originated. But we do know that evil will be completely wiped out one day, and until then we can overcome it in the name and power of

Yeshua, the Messiah. He is always ready to stand alongside us, give us supernatural power to overcome our enemy the devil and bring us out of the darkness and into the light. Just think about some of the "evil" acts committed by those who went on to become heroes of the faith.

The apostle Paul, who wrote more than half of the New Testament, persecuted and killed believers. Peter denied three times that he even knew Yeshua. David committed adultery with Uriah the Hittite's wife and then had the man killed to cover up his sin. You cannot get much more evil than that. And yet, if God had a Hall of Fame, every one of these men would have his photograph hanging there. Redemption is always possible—no matter what you have been through or what you have done. As the Bible says, "Now we know that all things work together for good for those who love God, who are called according to His purpose" (Romans 8:28).

God's love changes everything!

Sarah, the girl I told you about at the beginning of this chapter, watched her life turned upside down by hatred and evil. But it is slowly being rebuilt by those who follow the Bible's admonition, "Do not be overcome by evil, but overcome evil with good" (Romans 12:21). Several faith-based organizations are on the ground in Uganda and doing everything they can to bring God's love to children and families who have lost everything to war and violence. They are reaching out in the name of Jesus to ensure that boys and girls like Sarah have nutritious food to eat, clean water and medical care. They are providing sanitary latrines to prevent the spread of cholera, dysentery and other potentially deadly diseases. Schools are being built where kids like Sarah can get the tools they need to build a better life.

The same thing is happening all over the world. Where evil has caused pain and suffering, you will find people who have given their lives to Jesus working to remedy the situation: building hospitals, clinics and schools. Digging wells to bring clean, safe water to thirsty communities. Helping people break the cycle of poverty by providing livestock, seeds and farming tools, and teaching new farming techniques so people can grow more food. Many are working in dangerous areas that are torn by war and violence—putting their own lives on the line in order to help others.

Why do they do it? Because they are compelled by the love of God. Having experienced His love for themselves, they have dedicated their lives to sharing it with others. And evil cannot withstand the love of God.

We may never know exactly how evil came to be. But we can know for certain that it will soon be destroyed forever.

> Then I saw a new heaven and a new earth; for the first heaven and the first earth had passed away, and the sea was no more. I also saw the holy city—the New Jerusalem—coming down out of heaven from God, prepared as a bride adorned for her husband. I also heard a loud voice from the throne, saying, "Behold, the dwelling of God is among men, and He shall tabernacle among them. They shall be His people, and God Himself shall be among them and be their God. He shall wipe away every tear from their eyes, and death shall be no more. Nor shall there be mourning or crying or pain any longer, for the former things have passed away."
>
> Revelation 21:1–4

7

In Sickness and in Health

I have stood by the bedside of a woman whose
thighbone was eaten through with cancer and who
had thriving colonies of the disease in many other
bones as well. It took three people to move her in
bed. The doctors predicted a few months of life;
the nurses (who often know better) a few weeks.
A good man laid his hands on her and prayed. A
year later the patient was walking (uphill, too,
through rough woodland) and the man who took
the last X-ray photos was saying, "These bones
are as solid as a rock. It's miraculous."

C. S. Lewis[1]

The telephone call came early on a Monday morning.
The night before, Pastor John and several men of
his church had prayed for a man who was not healthy. They
were so desperate to see him healed that they prayed for two

hours. Pastor John had been leading healing prayer at his church for ten months, convinced that God wanted them to pray for the sick, but nobody had been healed. This time, same result. You can imagine how humiliated he was to see people walk away still sick and suffering. Some members had left the church, and others thought it was time to quit trying. That evening, John was brokenhearted to the point of throwing himself on the floor. "You tell us to believe in healing, and pray for healing, but You're not doing anything. Oh, God, it's not fair!" Trudging home, John fell into bed feeling defeated.

The next morning, he was awakened by the phone call. One of his new members wanted John to pray for his sick wife. Once John would have been happy to pray for the woman's healing, but after the last several months—after the evening before—John could not help but wonder if he was in for another disappointment.[2]

John's wife described what happened that morning when he obediently left to try again.

> When he got to the house, the woman's face was so red, and she was sweating so much, that John groaned inwardly, "Oh no, this looks like a hard one!" Muttering a faithless prayer, John quickly turned to the husband to explain why some people don't get healed. But before he could finish, the husband was grinning from ear to ear. His wife had got up looking like a different person. She even offered them some coffee. John drove away ecstatic, yelling at the top of his lungs, "We got one! It really works!" and celebrating the fact that God had used him as a vehicle of his healing mercy.[3]

"My despair from the previous night was instantly transformed into joy and exaltation," John later wrote. "The period of gestation was over; the healing ministry was born in me, at the moment I least expected it would be."[4]

You may have figured out that that the pastor in this story was John Wimber, the late leader of the Vineyard, a group of churches that places a very strong emphasis on healing.

Does God heal today? Yes. I believe beyond any doubt that He does.

When Healing Does Not Come

But why does everyone not get healed? And what was going on during those ten months when John Wimber was crying out to God for healing and there was no response?

Theologians and philosophers have been debating questions like these for decades. I am not so arrogant as to think I can fully answer them in a few pages. But I do believe that I have some particular insights that can help us gain a better understanding of why and how healing takes place.

My dear friend and Jewish Voice senior editor Larry Walker passed away from cancer this past winter. Despite our repeated prayer vigils over a twenty-month period and his deep faith in God's Word and conviction God would heal him, he was not healed.

A couple of days ago, I was talking to another friend who lost his wife to cancer at the age of 49. She left behind three children, including a son with special needs. She was involved in a Bible-believing church that prayed constantly for her healing. She was anointed with oil in obedience to James 5:14-16. She received messages from believing friends around the country who let her know they were praying fervently for her healing.

Some sent her audio tapes about healing, teaching that God has already provided the healing and it is up to us to grab hold of it. In other words, if I am not healed of something, it is because I did not have enough faith. Is this true? The Bible certainly seems to indicate that there is a correlation between healing and faith. And yet, it was when John Wimber's faith was at low tide that his first healing occurred.

And, despite her efforts to have more faith, my friend's wife died.

I have been in full-time ministry now for more than thirty years, and I have witnessed scores of deeply committed, faith-filled believers pass away prematurely from illnesses and unexpected tragedies. After all these years, I realize I know less now than I did when I started.

I do not understand why some get healed and some do not. Even more disconcerting is why some who do get healed are seemingly undeserving and have little or no faith, while others who do not get healed are some of the most faithful and dedicated followers of the Lord I have ever known.

What I do know, however, is that when I pray for people to be healed, I must believe that God desires to heal them, that it is God's will to heal "all who were oppressed by the devil" (Acts 10:38).

John Wimber often spoke of a vision God gave him as he drove home after that first healing. He saw honey dripping from heaven, and the people below were either weeping with joy, receiving it gladly or annoyed, trying to wipe it off. The Lord explained that the honey was His mercy, which for some would be a blessing and others a hindrance. But there would always be plenty to go around.[5]

Of those ten months when his church was asking for healing but seeing none, Wimber wrote that it was

> a time in which I was purged of my pride and self-sufficiency. . . .
> God had first to cleanse a vessel before it was fit to fill with his
> precious oil of healing. I believe God began healing the sick
> through me only after I came to a place of total dependence
> on his grace and mercy.[6]

Wimber knew his experience was not typical. He had seen many believers get amazing healings the first time they prayed for one. But God deals with each of us as individuals, and He may be doing a work in the healer's life just as much as in the life of the one being healed.

Anyone who wants to see the sick healed must pray with faith that it will happen. Mark 6 says that when Jesus visited His hometown of Nazareth, He could not do much there because of the people's lack of faith:

> When Shabbat came, He began to teach in the synagogue.
> Many listeners were amazed, saying, "Where did this fellow get
> these things? What's this wisdom given to Him? Such miracles
> are done by His hands! Isn't this the carpenter, the son of
> Miriam, and the brother of Jacob and Joseph and Judah and
> Simon? Aren't His sisters here with us?" And they took offense
> at Him. Then Yeshua began saying to them, "A prophet is not
> without honor except in his hometown, among his relatives,
> and in his own house." He was not able to do any miracle,
> except that He laid hands on a few sick people and healed
> them. And He was astonished because of their unbelief.
>
> Mark 6:2–6

That said, I think we sometimes misunderstand what is meant by "faith." We are not called to have faith in faith. Our faith is to be placed in God and God alone. Consider what happened to John Wimber. It was when he was at his weakest and most vulnerable that God responded in a miraculous way to his prayer. Only when Wimber was completely empty of his own pride and humble before God did a miracle of healing come. As God told the apostle Paul, "My grace is sufficient for you, for power is made perfect in weakness" (2 Corinthians 12:9). Again and again, when we come to the end of ourselves, we find God waiting there to help us.

Want to Heal the Sick? Pray

One of the requirements for experiencing God's healing power is actually praying for the sick! By this I mean stepping out in faith to pray for the sick. People may go through their prayer lists in private, but they are not bold enough to walk up to someone who needs healing, ask to pray for them and lay hands on them, praying right then and there. Jack Deere asks, "How often do you go into a hospital room and pray for the sick and suffering to be miraculously healed? How often do you lay your hands on the sick in your church and pray for them?"[7] He testifies that everyone he knows who steps out in faith this way experiences at least some healings. But remember that you by yourself do not have the power to heal. That power comes from the Spirit of God within you.

Why do we not pray for the sick the way Dr. Deere suggests? Because we are afraid that healing will not come, and then we will be embarrassed. And, sometimes, we are afraid that healing will not come and then God will be embarrassed. If God does not come through, then He will look bad and people might lose faith. I read about a group that was actually called Save Our Savior. They were upset about the way some movies, books and television shows portray Yeshua. And while I understand their point of view, I do not agree that our God needs anyone to save Him! God can take care of His own reputation. He does not need our help. He wants us to pray for the sick and let Him take care of the rest.

If you pray and nothing happens, keep on praying. Some people say they will pray only one time for healing, no more, because to pray any more than that demonstrates a lack of faith. But that is not the way I read it. Jesus told us to keep on knocking, seeking and asking until we get the answer we are looking for. In fact, He told the story of the unjust judge, who didn't really have compassion for people, but gave a widow the justice she was seeking, simply because she bothered him so much (see Luke 18:1–6). Jesus said, "And will not God bring about justice for his chosen ones, who cry out to him day and night? Will he keep putting them off? I tell you, he will see that they get justice, and quickly" (verses 7–8 NIV).

Be Willing to Take a Risk

Evangelist Robby Dawkins writes,

> Don't get discouraged if you pray for someone and healing doesn't happen, or if you must pray several times. God is not discouraged with you! Just ask yourself, *Do I want to see God heal the sick?* No one wins a war by firing a single bullet; it usually takes many shots. Persevere in praying for sick people, and I guarantee you'll see healing happen. If you want to see it happen even faster, pray for people outside the Church. Our simple acts of faith praying for healing in

the environment of the world are like a weapon of mass destruction against the kingdom of darkness.[8]

As an example, Dawkins shares about his son Judah, who was in a fast-food restaurant when he encountered another teen with a broken leg. He was walking on crutches and told Judah that the leg hurt any time he put pressure on it.

Judah told the other boy that Jesus could heal him and asked if he could pray for him. When the young man said yes, Judah called out to everyone in the restaurant and invited them to gather around and watch. About ten other young people came to see what was going on. One of them said, "I'm an atheist. I don't believe in this stuff."

Judah responded that if he was an atheist, he needed to get really close so he could see better. Then he began praying, and the boy with the broken leg said his pain level had dropped from a twelve down to a two. He prayed a second prayer and it dropped to zero.

> That young man began walking around without crutches, putting his full weight on the leg and having no pain whatsoever. Judah turned and looked at the group that had gathered around to watch. "Jesus healing this kid's leg was Him inviting you all to have a relationship with Him," he said. "Now, how would you like to respond to Jesus' invitation to you?" And all who saw, including that young atheist, were impacted for God.[9]

Unexpected Healing

In January 1990, Duane Miller lost his voice permanently. That would be bad for anyone, but Miller was a pastor. His vocal cords were severely damaged, and he was told that he would not get his voice back. Miller felt that he had no choice but to resign his pastorate. Of course, the members of his congregation were praying faithfully for his healing, but it seemed their prayers were getting no further than the ceiling of their church.

With the aid of a custom-designed microphone, Miller was able to at least teach a Sunday school class, though it gave him a terrible sore throat. One morning in January 1993, three years after losing his voice, Miller was leading his class in a study of Psalm 103. After reading verse 3, which declares that God is the One who "forgives all your sins and heals all your diseases" (NIV), Miller said that some people try to put God in a box, either by insisting that He does not heal today, or by insisting that He always heals in response to the prayer of faith. "But . . . He won't be put in a box."

Miller confessed he did not know why some are healed and others are not, but that we just have to trust the Lord's wisdom. As he began to read the next line of the psalm, his voice changed. He knew immediately that the feeling in his throat was completely different.

> I would love to tell you that I knew exactly what it was . . . and that I expected God to do it and wasn't surprised. But it would be a lie. It scared me to death. I stopped, startled, and then said two or three words, thinking "Am I hearing what I think I hear?" . . . I tried to get back to the lesson, but I couldn't and nobody cared. People began to applaud. Everybody was weeping. There were about two hundred in the class and there were no dry eyes. Somebody began to sing the doxology. Someone else said we had witnessed the power of God. We just thanked the Lord for what He had done.[10]

The Gift of Healing

I heard the following story from a retired preacher, Pastor Edwards, who shook his head and laughed at the memory.

"That was one of the strangest prayer requests I ever got," he chuckled.

It happened about thirty years ago, on a Sunday night at a church near Orlando, Florida. When Pastor Edwards asked anyone who needed prayer to come down to the altar, an elderly gentleman slowly made his way out of his pew and shuffled to the front. He moved slowly, deliberately, as if he was in great pain.

The pastor came over and asked him quietly, "What do you want me to ask the Lord to do for you?"

"I want you to pray that He'll help me get together two hundred dollars."

"Two hundred dollars?" Pastor Edwards repeated, taken aback that the man had not asked for prayer for the healing he obviously needed.

"That's right," said the elderly gentleman. "That's enough to buy a round-trip plane ticket to Tulsa, Oklahoma."

"Tulsa?"

"Yes, sir. Then when I get there I can go see Oral Roberts and have him pray for me so I can be healed!"

Pastor Edwards' eyes twinkled. "I guess he showed me what he thought of my ability to get an answer to prayer."

I admit, I thought the story was funny. But at the same time, I do believe that some people have special gifts of healing, like Oral Roberts and Kathryn Kuhlman, two of the best-known and most influential healing ministers of that day.

While I believe that all believers have the ability to pray in faith and see sick people healed, 1 Corinthians 12:6–11 says,

There are various kinds of working, but the same God who works all things in all people. But to each person is given the manifestation of the Ruach [Holy Spirit] for the benefit of all. For to one is given through the Ruach a word of wisdom, to another a word of knowledge according to the same Ruach, to another faith by the same Ruach, to another gifts of healings by the one Ruach, to another workings of miracles, to another prophecy, to another discerning of spirits, to another different kinds of tongues, to another the interpretation of tongues. But one and the same Ruach activates all these things, distributing to each person individually as He wills.

John Wimber writes that in the earlier days of his ministry, he and his wife, Carol, were angered by the "faith healers" they saw on television and would quickly change the channel if one came on the air.

Carol and I also visited several healing meetings and became angry with what appeared to be the manipulation of people for the material gains of the faith healer. Even when it appeared that some people were healed, we were not able to accept it as being from God; Jesus, we thought, would never make such a spectacle! Dressing like sideshow barkers, pushing people over and calling it the power of God, and money— they were always asking for more, leading people to believe that if they gave, they would be healed.[11]

The Wimbers eventually changed their minds about many of the "faith healers" they had once denigrated. This was mostly because they changed their minds regarding supernatural healing. Earlier on they subscribed to a theology which insisted that healings and other supernatural miracles had been done away with after the first century. (We will talk more about this theology in the next chapter.) They did not believe in supernatural healing, so they thought all "faith healers" were fakes.

They changed their minds about this for a number of reasons, including the fact that their three-year-old son, Sean, was healed through prayer after being stung repeatedly by a swarm of bees.

But even though the Wimbers softened their attitudes and came to appreciate some of the people they had disparaged, that does not mean there are no "phonies" in the healing business today. Which is nothing new—these people have been around since the first century. The apostle Paul wrote of them,

> Some are proclaiming the Messiah out of envy and strife, but others out of good will. The latter do so out of love, knowing that I am appointed for the defense of the Good News. The former proclaim Messiah not sincerely, but out of selfishness—expecting to stir up trouble for me in my imprisonment. But what does it matter? Only that in every way, whether in dishonesty or in truth, Messiah is being proclaimed—and in this I rejoice! Yes, and I will keep rejoicing.
>
> Philippians 1:15–18

The book of Acts also tells the story of a magician named Simon who wanted to buy the power of the Holy Spirit (Acts 8:9–24).

The very fact that frauds are out there verifies that some people really do have special gifts of healing from the Holy Spirit. For without the real thing, there would be nothing to counterfeit.

But how do you know if someone is truly anointed by God? Here are three important things I have learned during my journey of faith.

A true man or woman of God will proclaim Yeshua, rather than himself or herself.

If an evangelist and healer is constantly tooting his own horn, I would not put much faith in him. A good question to ask is, "Who is getting top billing here?" Believe me, I understand the need for marketing and fund-raising. Any national or international ministry that does not do these things will not survive. Still, the main thrust of a biblically based organization must be to lift up the Messiah and proclaim the salvation He offers.

Celebrity is not necessarily the mark of an effective, God-centered ministry.

Some people become famous because God does great things through them, because hundreds, even thousands, of people are set free from sickness and suffering through their ministries. Others become famous because they know how to build an organization and promote themselves. It is hard to tell, at first glance, which is taking place. I know many people who have received healing at crusades held by big-name preachers. But I sincerely believe that we will never know the names of most of the men and women who have been given gifts of healing. Most of them are serving quietly in their local churches and communities. They are not trying to hide the gifts God has given them but rather are serving where God has called them to serve. That is why the book of James says, "Is anyone among you sick? Let him call for the elders of Messiah's community, and let them pray over him, anointing him with oil in the name of the Lord. The prayer of faith will save the one who is sick, and the Lord will raise him up" (James 5:14–15).

A true man of God will preach the Word of God.

It is critical to evaluate everything you hear within the light of what the Bible says. Frankly, there are a lot of people out there who talk about Jesus but do not really serve Him. Some New Age healers use Scripture and talk about Jesus, but when you look beneath the surface, you can see that they do not really accept Him as Lord and Savior or the Bible as the authoritative Word of God. They may not even believe in God at all, but rather in "the God within." Yeshua said, "Not everyone who says to Me, 'Lord, Lord!' will enter the kingdom of heaven, but he who does the will of My Father in heaven."

Before we move on to our discussion of miracles, I want to touch on one more very important Bible verse about healing. James, the brother of Yeshua, instructs his readers, "Confess your offenses to one another and pray for one another so that you may be healed" (James 5:16).

God wants us to live in openness and honesty with one another and to pray for one another. He desires for His children to be together in a caring, sharing community of faith.

A friend of mine once told me about the day God impressed this on him and his wife. It seems he had a bad day at work and actually yelled at one of his co-workers. He felt bad about what he had done, especially because everybody at his workplace knew he was a Christian and he knew he had not been a good example of God's love.

When he got home that evening, his wife noticed right away that he was preoccupied. At the same time, he noticed that she seemed to be favoring her arm as she put the finishing touches on dinner.

"Are you okay?" he asked.

"I was just about to ask you the same question," she answered. "You first."

"No, you go first. What happened to your arm?"

She told him that she felt like she had pulled a muscle in her shoulder. "It's been hurting all day. I was going to ask you to pray for me."

"Of course," he said. "Let me do it right now."

"But I want to hear what's going on with you. Did something happen at work?"

"Oh, I was a jerk today," he said, and he proceeded to tell her about losing his temper with the co-worker.

His wife kissed him on the cheek and said, "You'll feel better after you apologize."

"I know. Now let me pray for you."

They sat down at the kitchen table and he took her hand in his. My friend told me that he did not really have much faith that God was going to answer his prayer, so he prayed for a long time, pleading with God to make it well. He did not want to get to the end of the prayer and hear his wife say, "It still hurts." But as soon as he finished, he looked up and saw a bright smile on her face.

"I couldn't wait for you to get to Amen," she said. "As soon as you started to pray, I felt something warm start in my shoulder and move down my entire arm. When it stopped, the pain was gone!"

They sat there for a moment, holding hands and thanking God for His mercy. Then he said, "I think maybe God has something to say to us."

He walked to his Bible, picked it up off the coffee table, opened it at random and began to read. "Therefore confess your sins to each other and pray for each other so that you may be healed" (James 5:16 NIV).

I do not recommend playing Bible roulette. God is under no obligation to speak to us when we do. But in this instance, I believe He was speaking clearly and giving a lesson we should all take to heart.

8

Miracles or Meshugas?

> There are only two ways to live your life. One is
> as though nothing is a miracle. The other is as
> though everything is a miracle.
>
> Albert Einstein

Seven-year-old Marie was beside herself. For the first time in her life, she was going to be late for school.

For some reason, nothing had been working right that morning. The buttons wouldn't stay buttoned. Her hair would not untangle. She had spilled her cereal on the kitchen floor.

Her big brother, who was known for his patience, had grown tired of waiting for her and left without her.

Finally, she was ready to go. If she hurried, she could still make it to class before the tardy bell rang. She snatched her lunch box off the table and ran out the door, heading toward the school two blocks away.

Marie knew that she was supposed to stop and look both ways before crossing the street. But this morning, she forgot. When she reached the curb, she kept going. Or, at least, tried to.

As she stepped into the street, she felt two strong hands on her shoulders, suddenly pushing her backward and out of the street. At that very moment, a car whizzed past, so close she could have touched it. She felt the *whoosh* of the wind, ruffling her hair as the vehicle sped past.

If Marie had taken one more step, she almost certainly would have been hit by that car. More than likely, she would have been seriously injured or even killed.

Was it a miracle that saved her life? Marie thinks so. That happened over forty years ago, and she has never doubted for a moment that God was watching over her that day. The memory remains clear and vivid. She shakes her head when asked if she is remembering the incident through the lens of a little girl's imagination.

"Absolutely not," she says. "I know what happened to me that morning." Marie goes on to explain that she had learned to love God from a very early age. She prayed every morning and night for His protection and blessing, and He gave it.

Genuine Miracles or . . . Meshugas?

What about you? Have you ever experienced a miracle? Or do you think people who claim to have experienced them are fooling themselves? The word *meshugas*, in case you do not know, is a Yiddish term for nonsense or craziness—what many people believe the idea of miracles to be.

Actually, I believe that *most* of us have experienced a miracle, but unless we keep our eyes open, we will not recognize one when it happens. That is because there almost always seems to be a "natural" explanation, especially for those who refuse to believe no matter what happens. And, frankly, some people would not believe in miracles even if they had been standing on the banks of the Red Sea when God parted the waters.

What do I mean by "natural explanation"? Several years ago, an acquaintance of mine who was a newspaper reporter had to cover a meeting in a part of his city that was filled with gangs. It was an area that seemed okay during the daytime, but when the sun went down, the entire complexion of the neighborhood changed.

The sky was just turning dark as my friend came out of his meeting. He walked briskly to where he had parked his car, got inside, put his key in the ignition and turned it.

Nothing.

He waited a minute or two and tried again.

Still nothing.

He did not know what to do. He did not have his cell phone with him, nor was he a member of AAA.

He was, however, a believer who knew that God could do great things. He got out of his car, laid his hands on the hood and began to pray. "Dear Lord, will You please start my car?" He continued to pray like that for a minute or two, and then, feeling rather silly about it, he got back in the driver's seat and turned the ignition.

The engine roared to life.

Shaking his head in wonder, and thanking God for performing a miracle, my friend slowly backed out of the parking space and headed for home.

The next morning, he took the car to a mechanic to get it checked out and was told it needed a new starter.

He insists that he did not tell anyone about laying hands on the car, but as the mechanic was giving him the diagnosis, he said, "You know, sometimes when the starter is going bad, if you just rock the car a little bit, you'll unlock a stuck gear and it will start right up."

What do you think? Was it a miracle or a coincidence? Did God start the car, or was it a lucky accident? As I said, that is often the way it is with miracles. God does something supernatural and the world says, "I can give you a natural explanation for that."

Another acquaintance of mine was driving in an unfamiliar part of town and pulled off the highway to get his bearings. After sitting there for a couple of moments, he prepared to get back on the road. He did not see any other cars coming in his rearview mirror, but for some reason—at the last minute—he hit the brakes and stopped just before he pulled back onto the pavement. In that instant, a big rig roared past. Had he not stopped, he would have been flattened by that truck.

Most of us have had experiences like that. Again, the question is, are they supernatural or merely natural? For the most part, I vote for the former.

I remember one time, not long after I took over leadership of Jewish Voice, when I became extremely discouraged and was thinking seriously about resigning. I had taken over after the former president, Louis Kaplan, died, and I had begun to think there was no way I could measure up to the standard he had set.

I could not seem to please anyone—especially my staff, who never hesitated to remind me, "That's not how Brother K. did it." Kaplan's widow, Chira, invited me to dinner, and I poured out my heart to her. "I'll never be able to fill Brother Kaplan's shoes," I said.

She listened politely, then excused herself and told me she would be right back. She went into her bedroom, and came out with three shoe boxes, each with a brand-new pair of shoes that her husband had bought but never worn. She told me that she had meant to give these shoes to me before but had forgotten to do it.

Now, I thought it was a nice gesture, but I doubted those shoes would fit me. I have very wide feet, and my shoe size is 8½ EEE. You could have knocked me over with a feather when I looked inside those shoes and saw what size they were. That is right—8½ EEE.

That may not sound like much of a miracle to you. But it certainly was to me! God had done something very specific to show me that, with His help, I could indeed fill Louis Kaplan's shoes and provide the leadership Jewish Voice needed. How like our God!

I believe that hundreds of "small" miracles like this happen every day. They are personal messages from God to His people, and there may not be any evidence at all to prove that they really happened. I cannot prove to you that the story I told you about Louis Kaplan's shoes happened just the way I said it did. If you know me, then you already know that I am an honest person who does not exaggerate, and you will be more inclined to believe me. Still, in the end, you just have to take my word for it.

Some miracles are irrefutable. You cannot deny it when people are healed of cancer, rescued from hopeless situations or raised from the dead. Sammy Hellman was my tour guide in Israel for more than thirty years, until he retired several years ago. I often witnessed to Sammy about my faith and challenged him to believe. One time he confided in me about guiding a group from a black Pentecostal church in the United States. Sammy was not expecting to see a miracle on the morning he went to pick up the group at their hotel in Jerusalem, but that is what happened.

He told me, "Out of the corner of my eye, I saw an elderly, gray-haired woman stumble on the top step. Before anyone could help her, she tumbled all the way down a flight of ten or twelve concrete steps. . . . It was a terrible fall. I knew she was badly injured."

Sammy ran over to see if he could help. She seemed to be unconscious, so he took her pulse and found none.

"She was dead," Sammy recounted. "Beyond any shadow of a doubt." Sammy, who had fought in two wars, told me that he knows what death looks like. "And she was dead."

The woman's pastor was the next person to reach her. He knelt down by her, began gently stroking her hair and prayed that the Lord would heal her. Then he spoke directly to the evidently dead woman. "Get up, Mrs. Wilson. You are not supposed to leave us. You are not supposed to disappoint Jesus, because He brought you here. He was the One who wanted to share with you His homeland. Now you are going to stand! Now you are going to stand!"

The woman's arm began to twitch. She slowly sat up and called out for someone to bring her purse, which she had dropped as she fell. She stood up, brushed herself off and insisted she was fine. Apparently she was! She spent the entire day touring the Holy City, without as much as a limp.

My friend shook his head and tears welled up as he recalled what he saw that day. "I was sure she had passed away. There was no doubt about it. I was 150 percent sure."

As the Bible says, "With God all things are possible" (Matthew 19:26).

Miracles in the Bible

For years, most Bible scholars insisted that miracles do not exist. That was their starting point as they studied the Bible, and in commentaries they explained away every supernatural experience in it. This presupposition was championed by the German school of higher criticism in the late nineteenth century and early twentieth century, which has greatly influenced Western theology to this day.

C. S. Lewis wrote about this mindset in his book *Miracles*:

> In a popular commentary on the Bible . . . the author says it must have been written after the execution of St. Peter, because in the Fourth Gospel, Jesus is represented as predicting the execution of St. Peter. "A book," thinks the author, "cannot be written *before* events which it refers to." Of course it cannot—unless real predictions ever occur. If they do, then this argument for the date is in ruins. And the author has not discussed at all whether real predictions are possible. . . . He has brought his disbelief in predictions to his historical work, so to speak, ready made.[1]

Lewis goes on to describe two types of people: naturalists, who believe that everything that happens is brought about by nature, because nature is all that exists; and supernaturalists, who believe that something more than nature exists.

> Naturalism, without ceasing to be itself, could admit a certain type of God. The great interlocking event called Nature might be such as to produce at some stage a great cosmic

129

consciousness, an indwelling "God" arising from the whole process. . . . What Naturalism cannot accept is the idea of a God who stands outside Nature and made it.[2]

Lewis says that he might be more inclined to doubt the reality of miracles if they were just an add-on to faith in Yeshua. Instead, a belief in miracles is central to our faith.

We believe that God sent His Son to earth to be born as a human baby. That is a miracle. We believe that Yeshua took upon Himself the sins of all mankind. That is another miracle. We believe He rose from the tomb on the third day after His death. Yet another miracle. Anyone who says that he or she has faith in Yeshua must believe that miracles happen. You cannot have one without the other.

Lewis, who wrote *The Lion, the Witch and the Wardrobe*, *The Great Divorce*, *Out of the Silent Planet* and many other classic works of fiction, also looked at miracles from the perspective of a novelist. Suppose you are reading a novel that has nothing at all to do with miracles or the supernatural, and the main character gets himself into a predicament he cannot seem to escape. All of a sudden, God swoops down out of nowhere with a fantastic miracle to get him out of trouble. First of all, you would be disappointed that the writer used such a lazy means of solving the hero's difficult situation. And you would not believe the miracle because it came out of the blue. There was no precedent for it. Not so with the story that is told in the Bible; it is a miraculous tale from the start. Lewis writes,

> Some people probably think of the Resurrection as a desperate last moment expedient to save the Hero from a situation which had got out of the Author's control. The reader may

set his mind at rest. If I thought miracles were like that, I should not believe in them. If they have occurred, they have occurred because they are the very thing the universal story is about. They are not exceptions (however rarely they occur) nor irrelevancies. They are precisely those chapters in this great story on which the plot turns.[3]

Are Miracles for Today?

One popular teaching is that the age of miracles has passed. They were okay in the first century, but not today. This teaching is based on 1 Corinthians 13, which says,

> Love never fails—but where there are prophecies, they will pass away; where there are tongues, they will cease; where there is knowledge, it will pass away. For we know in part and we prophesy in part; but when that which is perfect has come, then that which is partial will pass away.
>
> 1 Corinthians 13:8–10

It is taught that "that which is perfect" is referring to the Bible. Now that we have the Bible, we no longer have a need for miracles and supernatural gifts, so they have all passed away. But if you keep reading, verse 12 says, "For now we see in a mirror dimly, but then face to face." It seems clear to me that this passage of Scripture is referring to the Messiah's return to earth as King of kings and Lord of lords. When Yeshua returns in glory, everything will be set right on this earth. There will be no more violence, heartbreak or desperate situations, and thus no need for miracles.

The last thing I ever want to be is judgmental or harsh. But I wonder if some people do not turn to 1 Corinthians to justify their lack of faith. They do not have miracles in their own lives, so they look at Paul's words and say, "Oh, this is the reason I never see any miracles. They're not for today!"

Then, too, if you do not believe in miracles, you will not get them.

Every believer should constantly be on the lookout for miracles. If we do not get them, something is wrong. Perhaps we need to ask God for more faith, or to open our eyes so we can see. (As I mentioned before, I believe many "small" miracles happen every day, but most of us miss them because we are not looking for them.) Or it could be that unconfessed sin is standing between us and God.

Now, I am not saying there is anything wrong if some of your prayers go unanswered. There are times when God says no. We may pray for someone to be healed from cancer, and he or she dies anyway. We ask Him to set us free from some difficult situation, and He does not do it. Yeshua warned us that we would go through difficult times (see John 16:33). The apostle Paul prayed three times that his "thorn in the flesh" would be taken from him, but God said no (2 Corinthians 12:7–10). But again, if we never see a miraculous answer to prayer, something is wrong somewhere. We cannot just throw up our hands and say, "Oh, well. I guess that's just the way it is."

Jesus said,

> Ask, and it shall be given you; seek, and ye shall find; knock, and it shall be opened unto you: For every one that asketh receiveth; and he that seeketh findeth; and to him that knocketh it shall be opened. Or what man is there of you, whom if his son ask bread, will he give him a stone? Or if he ask a fish, will he give him a serpent? If ye then, being evil, know

how to give good gifts unto your children, how much more shall your Father which is in heaven give good things to them that ask him?

Matthew 7:7–11 KJV

We must learn to live in joyful expectation of what God is going to do, being willing to accept His will at all times.

Jesus taught us to pray that God's will be done on earth as it is in heaven. Obviously, it is extremely important to seek God's will and to strive to make sure that our prayers line up with His will. I hear many prayers that include the phrase "if it be Your will." "Heavenly Father, please heal her, if it be Your will." "Dear God, please give me more faith, if it be Your will." And so on.

We have to be careful not to use that phrase to cover up our own lack of faith. Do we say, "If it be Your will," because we are afraid God will not respond the way we want Him to? Do we think He is not listening to us?

Two Who Changed Their Minds

Miracles will come when we pray in faith!

Saint Augustine was one of those who believed that the age of miracles had passed. When he was a young man, he believed that they had occurred in the early days of the Church to affirm the truth of the Gospel but that they had since been taken away. In his later years, he changed his mind. In fact, in *The City of God* (book 22.8), he said that in a two-year period more than seventy miracles had been recorded and verified in his city of Hippo. What changed? Nothing, except that Augustine kept his eyes open and was willing to change his mind. God performed miracles in the first century and the fifth century, and He performs them today.

Dr. Jack Deere also once believed that the age of miracles was past. As an associate professor of Old Testament at Dallas Theological Seminary and pastor in a church in Fort Worth that he had helped start, he had never experienced a miracle or known anyone who had, and he was perfectly fine with this. He believed this was the way God intended it.

That changed when he invited one of his favorite authors, Dr. John White, to speak at a Bible conference at his church. Deere assumed Dr. White felt the same way about the absence of miracles in the modern world as he did. But during the conference, Dr. White invited people to come to the front of the church for prayer for spiritual needs, which was unheard of in Dr. Deere's church. Also unheard of was the response: Around a hundred people rushed to the front, even people Deere had thought to be strong, healthy Christians. He was especially surprised to see an articulate and intelligent woman he had known for years approach him, begging for relief from a desire for other people's approval that had taken over her life. Deere and some elders prayed for her, and absolutely nothing happened. Moments later, he witnessed Dr. White taking authority over a demon that had been tormenting her and had started moving her body in ways she could not control. Deere had never seen anything like it. He wrote,

> While I watched her being tormented, I thought of all the wasted years she had spent in Christian counseling without having any significant improvement. . . . I felt tears running down my cheeks as I realized the damage arrogant pastors like myself can inflict on the Lord's children. . . . Demons really come out by the power of the blood of Christ. Until

John White came along, none of her pastors or counselors
had the discernment to realize what was the root cause of
Linda's afflictions, so Linda had "suffered much at the hands
of her physicians."[4]

Now, I do believe there are times when people who are
suffering with personal and spiritual problems do get better through counseling. I have seen people make huge turn-
arounds in their lives by spending more time in prayer, becoming more disciplined in the study of God's Word and
fellowshiping with other believers. But there are also situations like Linda's, where only a miracle direct from the hand
of God will set a person free. The key in every situation is
to be discerning and ask God to show us what is required.
Then we must be open to whatever He tells us.

Believe and Receive

I have personally seen many supernatural healings over my
years of ministry. A great many have occurred in developing
nations like India, Ethiopia and Zimbabwe, where Jewish
Voice provides free medical clinics. Many who come to us
have illnesses and ailments that cannot be treated medically.
I have seen people healed of AIDS, cancer and other terminal
illnesses. I have seen sight restored to the blind, deaf ears
opened and the lame walk. In fact, I have seen just about
everything but a dead person resurrected—although I have
met people who have witnessed this, and I have been praying
for this experience.

In Gondar, Ethiopia, we have been providing free medical,
dental and eye care to the Beta Israel tribe since 1999. (Beta
Israel is Hebrew for "House of Israel.") These are Jews who

may well be descendants of the lost tribe of Dan. Although 130,000 of them now live in Israel, many were left behind because they were labeled *Mora*, those who at some point in their family history converted to Orthodox Christianity. Tens of thousands remain in Ethiopia.

They are among the poorest of the poor, living in isolation and squalor. Shunned by their fellow countrymen, they are disdained and persecuted, for their superstitious neighbors believe they are *buda*, possessors of the "evil eye" who turn into hyenas by night. According to legend, when transformed they steal children and drink their blood. When something bad happens in the region, like a drought or illness, the Beta Israel are blamed. It is very similar to the blood libels in Eastern Europe during the Middle Ages, although I can find no direct historical connection between the two.

I remember one particular young man in his early twenties who came to us for help back in 2011. He had been born deaf and had never spoken. We were treating members of this community for several days, helping as many as we could medically and inviting them to receive prayer after their treatment. I was standing in the courtyard when I heard excited voices coming from the prayer tent. Some of our volunteers came out with the young man, all of them rejoicing together.

They excitedly explained that because there was no medical help available for the young man, our prayer team had laid hands on him and commanded his ears to open. The tangible presence of God filled the prayer tent, and his ears were opened. He could hear!

I wanted to check this out for myself, so I positioned myself behind the boy and whispered into his right ear, "Yeshua."

With a moaning tone, but clearly, he repeated my word, "Yeshua." I then whispered into his left ear "Praise the Lord." Again, he clearly repeated back what I had said. Everyone was amazed. The elders of the community who witnessed this miracle were visibly shaken. They had known the young man since his birth and knew that he had always been deaf. His healing reminded me of the story from Acts 3 about the beggar lame from birth healed at the gate of the Temple called Beautiful. Yes, we serve a God of miracles!

Why Do Miracles Exist?

If we follow the evidence with an open mind, I believe we must come to the conclusion that miracles are real, and that they exist today. They are rare, of course; if they were commonplace, they would not be miracles.

At the same time, there are what we might call "natural miracles" that happen millions of times every day within each human body. Every time we take a breath, make a movement or have a thought, many thousands of processes are involved, and they all occur with pinpoint precision. More biologists and physicists are coming to a belief in God as they discover the amazing complexity of human life. This complexity may not be "miraculous" in the pure sense of the word. But, clearly, the Creator who designed it all so that it works seamlessly is certainly capable of impacting the laws of nature to bring about what we might call "supernatural" miracles.

We have seen that miracles happen. But why do they happen? Why does God give them? I believe there are at least four important reasons.

God gives miracles because He has compassion on us.
Luke 7:11–15 says,

> The next day Yeshua traveled to a town called Nain, and coming along with Him were His disciples and a large crowd. Just as He came near the town gate, behold, a dead man was being carried out, the only son of his mother, a widow. A considerable crowd from the town was with her. When the Lord saw her, He felt compassion for her and said, "Don't cry." Then He came up and touched the coffin, and the pallbearers came to a standstill. He said, "Young man! I tell you, get up!" The dead man sat up and began speaking, and Yeshua gave him to his mother.

There are a number of similar stories throughout the gospels. Yeshua had compassion on people who were hungry, sick, blind, lost and bereaved. He performed miracles because He cared about them, and He performs miracles today because He cares about you and me.

The poor woman in the story above had lost her only son. Jesus understood the heartbreak of a grieving parent and was moved to perform a miracle for her. He still understands when we are going through heartache and loss.

John 11 tells how Jesus raised His friend Lazarus from the dead. Verse 35 of that chapter is the shortest in the Bible: "Yeshua wept."

The Bible does not tell us why He wept, although we are told that He was "deeply moved" when He saw Lazarus' sister Miriam and her friends weeping at Lazarus' grave. I have heard it suggested that He wept because He was grieved that Lazarus was going to be brought back into this world of sin, sorrow and disappointment. But I think it is more likely that He was feeling the grief of His friends Miriam and Martha. His heart was broken because their hearts were broken. Perhaps He cried because He was thinking about all the sorrow and grief that death brings to this earth—about all the times when what He was witnessing that day would be repeated, as friends and families gather, weeping, around the graves of their loved ones.

So, again, the first reason God gives miracles is that He loves us and hates to see us suffer.

That does not mean He is going to give us everything we want, or perform miracle after miracle to keep us out of trouble. God is not an indulgent parent who delights in spoiling His children. His goal is for us to be the best people we can possibly be, and that means that most likely we will have to go through some difficult times. James, Yeshua's brother, put it this way: "Consider it all joy, my brethren, when you encounter various trials, knowing that the testing of your faith produces endurance. And let endurance have its perfect work, so that you may be perfect and complete, lacking in nothing" (James 1:2–4).

Jack Deere reminds us that

> God may allow suffering to come to us for a variety of reasons other than judgment for our sin. Job was considered by God the most righteous and blameless man on earth, yet God allowed Job to suffer horribly. . . . I find all too often that many of God's children mistakenly assume that their afflictions are evidence of God's judgment on them.[5]

We have the assurance that "now we know that all things work together for good for those who love God, who are called according to His purpose" (Romans 8:28).

If it takes a miracle to make things work together for your good, then God will give it.

God gives miracles to confirm His Word.

There are several passages in Scripture that tell us God gives "signs and wonders" to confirm the message of salvation through faith in Yeshua. In Mark 16:20, for example, after Yeshua's ascension, the disciples went out and preached "everywhere, the Lord working with them and confirming the word by the signs that follow." Acts 14:3 says, "So they [Paul and Barnabas] stayed there [in Iconium] a considerable time, speaking boldly in the Lord—who was testifying to the message of His grace, granting signs and wonders to come about by their hands."

In Romans 15:18–19, Paul says,

> For I will not dare to speak of anything except what Messiah accomplished through me, to bring about the obedience of the Gentiles by word and deed, in the power of signs and wonders, in the power of the Spirit of God. So from Jerusalem and around even to Illyricum, I have fully proclaimed the Good News of Messiah.

And finally, the writer of Hebrews says that God confirmed the truth of the message of salvation through the Messiah by "testifying by signs and wonders and various miracles" (Hebrews 2:4).

There are many verses that speak of signs and wonders validating the ministry and message of Jesus; see Matthew 9:6–7, Luke 11:20, John 3:2, John 9:32–33 and Matthew 12:26–28 for a few examples.

I believe that the same thing is happening today, especially in Africa and Asia, where millions have never even heard the name of Jesus, and in the Middle East, where Islamic State terrorists are torturing and killing people who refuse to convert to Islam.

According to Baptist Press, a Christian relief team in Lebanon has heard many stories about Jesus appearing to refugees who have been driven from their homes by the vicious fighting in Syria. The team recently brought food to a needy widow dressed for mourning and her three children. Though she was supposed to remain in isolation during the forty days of mourning, she invited them inside. Then, to their great surprise, she removed her veil, "unheard of in her conservative Muslim culture."

The night before, she said, "as I was sleeping, someone put His hand on my shoulder. He said, 'You don't know Me. You have passed through a great pain. I experienced a great pain, also. But I will not leave you alone. Tomorrow I will send you someone who will tell you about Me. Listen to him.'" She turned to the team leader and said, "Tell me about this person that I saw in my dream."

In tears, the man told her about Jesus, the friend of widows, orphans and outcasts. "This Book that I'm going to give you will explain to you about God's love," he promised, giving her a Bible along with a supply of food.[6]

In another story, a man was in his office when someone he described as "a beautiful man" suddenly appeared and told him that he needed to leave immediately. "You're in danger," the man told him. "Leave now."

The businessman rushed outside just as a bomb exploded, turning his office into a pile of rubble. A few days later the "beautiful man" returned in a vision. The businessman asked who He was and received the same answer as the apostle Paul: "I am Jesus" (Acts 9:5).[7]

A reporter named David Rupert writes,

By the thousands—or more—Muslims are receiving direct divine intervention through visions and dreams of Jesus himself.

I'm not a signs and wonders guy and have a healthy degree of skepticism. But who am I to say that God won't reach people any way He wants behind the Crescent Curtain. One missionary in the field told me, "It happens so often that we don't even question it."[8]

Most of the news we hear these days is discouraging—especially the news that comes from the Middle East and other parts of the world where Islamic extremists have unleashed a wave of terror. But in the midst of the bombings, mass shootings, beheadings and other brutal acts, God is at work. He has still got the whole world in His hands, and He is still confirming the truth of His Word with signs and wonders.

God gives miracles to confirm your salvation.

After God rescued the Israelites from Egypt, He gave them miracle after miracle as they journeyed toward the Promised Land. He parted the Red Sea so they could pass safely through the waters. He provided a cloud to lead them during the day and a pillar of fire to go before them at night. He gave them water from a rock and fed them with manna from heaven. He kept their clothes and shoes from wearing out. He did everything but carry them on His back.

But a time was coming when the children of Israel were going to have to stand on their own feet and fight for their survival. The land God had promised them was full of people who had no intention of giving it up. They had built great cities, like Jericho, and put together well-armed, well-trained armies that were ready to repel invaders.

Of course, God would be with the Israelites, just as He had always been—but He was not going to defeat their enemies with fire and brimstone or blow them away with one breath from His mouth. The time had come for the Israelites to walk by faith and not by sight. This would continue after they had built their new homes in the Promised Land. God had promised them a land flowing with milk and honey, but He did not milk the cows for them or tend the bees and harvest the honey. God expected them to do their share, to uphold their part of the covenant.

I believe the same thing happens to those who follow the Lord today. I believe it because I have experienced it, and because many people have told me that the same happened to them. Perhaps you have experienced it, too.

What a thrill to come to know Jesus the Messiah as your Lord and Savior! Suddenly life has a purpose and the days are filled with joy. At the same time, Satan wants you back, and he will do everything he can to get you to doubt your salvation. He wants to make you think that you just got carried away by emotion, that what happened to you was not real. He may even tell you that there is no heaven or hell, no supernatural realm, and that this world is all there is. But no matter how many darts he shoots at you, he cannot get through because God is walking alongside you and protecting you. It is a wonderful time of being held in God's hands. You do not feel that anything can go wrong, and even if it does, you know beyond doubt that God will take care of it.

During this period, life is filled with miracles. They may not be as great as some of the miracles you read about in the Bible, but they are miracles all the same. And even in the Bible, not all miracles were on par with raising the dead, healing the sick or parting the Red Sea. Yeshua's first miracle involved turning water into wine at a wedding. Some

143

miracles are smaller than others, but they are miracles just the same.

A friend told me that not long after she came to faith in Yeshua, she was on the freeway, driving alone in the middle of nowhere, miles from the nearest city—and she knew nothing about car engines.

Suddenly, she heard a booming noise and her car began to lose power. She pulled to the right and hoped she could keep rolling long enough to reach the off-ramp just ahead. She did, coasting all the way to the bottom of the exit and into a full-service gas station "way out there in the middle of the boonies!" There, she met an honest mechanic who explained that her fan belt had broken. Within a matter of minutes, her car was fixed and she was back on her way.

Perhaps that does not sound like a great off-ramp miracle to you, but it was to her. It showed her that God really does love her and is taking care of her. Countless things like this happen in the life of a believer, and although I am not saying they will not happen on a daily basis, I think they tend to occur more frequently in the early days of a relationship with God. And when they do, it is important to remember them, think about them and talk about them with other believers. That way, those events become entrenched in our minds, and they will always be there to remind us that God loves us and that nothing is going to happen to us that He cannot handle!

As God told the Israelites,

> Only be watchful and watch over your soul closely, so you do not forget the things your eyes have seen and they slip from your heart all the days of your life. You are to make them known to your children and your children's children.
>
> Deuteronomy 4:9

And again,

> Then ADONAI said to Moses, "Go to Pharaoh, because I have hardened his heart and the heart of his servants, so that I might show these My signs in their midst, and so you may tell your son and your grandchildren what I have done in Egypt, as well as My signs that I did among them, so you may know that I am ADONAI."
>
> Exodus 10:1–2

We must guard against two important things: If we are complacent—taking God's favor and mercy for granted—or if we are discontent with what He is doing for us, we won't see miracles happen in our lives.

The Israelites displayed both of these attitudes. From the day they left Egypt, they began to whine and moan, asking Moses if he had brought them into the desert to die of starvation or thirst. When God supplied manna, they complained that they had to eat the same old thing day after day. They did not seem to appreciate anything God did for them and talked about their lives of slavery in Egypt as if that had been the good old days.

They were ready to trade the blessings of life lived in the supernatural for the physical blessings that come from life in this world.

What do we do if we need a miracle, but God seems far away? First, I always examine myself to make sure that my relationship with God is in good shape. Is there any unconfessed sin in my life? Have I begun to take God's blessings lightly or been ungrateful for His mercy and grace? Have I become complacent or ungrateful? If so, I confess to God and ask for His forgiveness, knowing that "if we confess our sins,

He is faithful and righteous to forgive our sins and purify us from all unrighteousness" (1 John 1:9).

If I can honestly say that there is nothing standing between God and me, if I have done everything I can to ensure that the relationship is strong and healthy, but God still does not answer my prayers, I assume that He wants me to walk in faith, trusting Him for the best possible outcome. After all, His ways are not our ways and His thoughts are not our thoughts. But He promises us in Jeremiah 29:11, "For I know the plans that I have in mind for you . . . plans for shalom and not calamity—to give you a future and a hope."

God knows best. Some of the greatest miracles I have ever had were the ones He did not give me. Looking back, I can see many times when I asked for something that would not have been good for me. I can see how difficult times increased my faith and made me a stronger, better person.

Remember, God always knows what is best for you. If you seek Him with a pure and humble heart, He will provide what is best.

God gives miracles to announce the arrival of His Kingdom.

A fourth important reason miracles occur is that they show the reality and power of God's Kingdom. When Yeshua appeared before Pilate, He was asked if He was king of the Jews.

> Yeshua answered, "My kingdom is not of this world. If My kingdom were of this world, then My servants would be fighting so that I wouldn't be handed over to the Judean leaders. But as it is, My kingdom is not from here." So Pilate said to

Him, "Are you a king, then?" Yeshua answered, "You say that I am a king. For this reason I was born, and for this reason I came into the world."

John 18:36–37

There is a supernatural Kingdom, and it is greater in every way than the kingdoms of the world.

There are dozens of references to the Kingdom of God in the New Testament, at least fifty of them in the book of Matthew alone.

Before Yeshua ascended to heaven, He told the apostles to wait in Jerusalem until they received power from on high (Acts 1:4–8). The event Yeshua was talking about occurred fifty days later and turned the city of Jerusalem upside down. Acts 2 tells the story:

> When the day of Shavuot had come, they [the disciples] were all together in one place. Suddenly there came from heaven a sound like a mighty rushing wind, and it filled the whole house where they were sitting. And tongues like fire spreading out appeared to them and settled on each one of them. They were all filled with the Ruach ha-Kodesh and began to speak in other tongues as the Ruach enabled them to speak out. Now Jewish people were staying in Jerusalem, devout men from every nation under heaven. And when this sound came, the crowd gathered. They were bewildered, because each was hearing them speaking in his own language.
>
> Acts 2:1–6

That was the first great outpouring of the New Covenant. Peter preached the first Gospel sermon, and 3,000 Jews came to faith in Yeshua. The Kingdom had arrived in great power.

There are numerous other passages in which the arrival of God's Kingdom is equated with miracles.

Matthew 4:23 says, "Yeshua was going throughout all the Galilee, teaching in their synagogues and proclaiming the Good News of the kingdom, and healing every kind of disease and sickness among the people."

Luke 10 tells of a time when Yeshua sent seventy people out across Israel as His representatives. He told them, "Whatever town you enter and they welcome you, eat what they set before you. Then heal the sick in that town, and say to them, 'The kingdom of God has come near to you'" (verses 8–9).

Acts 8:6–12 also talks about miracles that occurred after Stephen proclaimed "the good news about the Kingdom of God."

In his best-selling book *Eternity in Their Hearts*, Don Richardson tells an amazing story of how the Kingdom of God took root in northern Burma and China. In 1887 a missionary named William Marcus Young moved from the United States to Burma and began preaching in an isolated, mostly uncharted part of the country called the Shan States. Young was, by all accounts, a passionate man who prayed fervently for souls to be won to God's Kingdom, and he had great success preaching to the Lahu people.

About three hundred kilometers to the north lived a fierce tribe of headhunters known as the Wa. Among this tribe of warriors and opium growers lived a man named Pu Chan who followed a different way of life. According to Richardson, Pu Chan was a descendant of a long line of prophets who worshiped "the true God." He was respected by the Wa and had a number of disciples, although the majority of the tribe ignored him when he told them, "Stop getting drunk!" and "It's wrong to sleep with other men's wives" and "Your headhunting is evil."

Pu Chan and the prophets who came before him had told the Wa people that the true God would be revealed to them through a white brother. One day, after hours spent in prayer, Pu Chan told his disciples that the time had come to meet this white brother. He saddled a little pony, turned it out of the village and told his disciples to follow it. It would lead them to the "white brother bearing the book of Siych, the true God."

Those men followed that little pony for hours over rugged mountainous trails and finally down into the town of Kengtung, where Young had built a small mission. The pony turned into the gate of that mission and headed straight for a water well. There it stopped.

The Wa tribesmen were puzzled and disappointed. There was no white brother in sight. Could the prophet have made a mistake?

Richardson writes,

Nelda Widlund, daughter of Vincent Young and granddaughter of William Marcus Young, told me in person what happened next. For she was raised on that very mission compound, and drank often from that very well. The details which follow form a treasured memory of the entire Young clan: The Wa tribesmen heard sounds in the well. They looked inside it and saw no water, but only two clear blue eyes looking up at them out of a friendly, bearded white face.

"Hello, strangers!" The voice—speaking in the Shan language—echoed out of the well. "May I help you?" William Marcus Young climbed out of the well, which was not yet in use (he was still in the process of digging it). As he brushed the dust from his hands and faced them, the Wa messengers asked, "Have you brought a book of God?"

Young nodded, reached into his shirt pocket and pulled out a small copy of the Bible. The Wa men, overcome with emotion, fell at his feet. "This pony is saddled especially for you," they told him. "Our people are all waiting. Fetch the book! We must be on our way!"[9]

Over the next few years, 10,000 Wa came to faith in Yeshua and were baptized. These converts helped spread the Gospel throughout eastern Burma and southwestern China.

Yes, amazing things do happen in this world. God is still in the miracle-working business.

9

More Than Fairy Tales

After my Near-Death Experience . . . I was obsessed with returning to heaven. The beauty, wonder, joy and love of heaven were my heart's desire,
and I had a case of terminal homesickness. . . .
What could the world have to offer that wasn't
infinitely better in heaven?

Howard Storm[1]

If you believe in heaven, you have plenty of company.
Depending on the poll you look at, somewhere between
72 percent and 83 percent of Americans do.[2] And most of
those questioned in a survey believed that they will be among
those accepted into the company of the saints and angels
after they die. Of those who believe in hell, fewer than 1
percent believe they will be sent to that place of torment
and damnation.

So what is the reality? Is there a heaven? If there is, where is it and how do we get there? Is it hiding behind another universe, or are our feeble eyes simply unable to see its magnificence while we still live? What will we find when we get there? And what does it look like?

Different cultures around the globe and throughout time have envisioned heaven in a myriad of ways. Vikings believed feasting and drinking and a nonstop good time awaited them in Valhalla. Islam teaches of a heaven as physical as the earth, where wants and wishes are immediately granted and existence is as abundant and luxurious as an oasis. Buddhists believe that a variety of heavens exist, tailored to how people have lived their lives. A warrior, for example, who has fought for good will go to one kind of realm; a teacher to another. But, for the Buddhist, paradise is not eternal; eventually one must rejoin the cycle of life and, by doing good, accumulate more karma.

Just as diverse are different cultures' conceptions of the path to heaven. If you had been a citizen of ancient Rome, you would have believed that two magnificent white steeds would whisk you there in a blazing chariot. Religions in the Far East saw their heaven, Nirvana, as the culmination of a cycle of birth and rebirth for every soul, each birth an opportunity to do good and accumulate good karma. The Egyptians of long ago believed the way to paradise was only achieved through an arduous journey, both dangerous and lonely. That was why Egyptians buried food, wine, beautiful treasured belongings—some to be given to the gods—and even slaves to accompany the departed.

Jews, however, believed just the opposite. The only accompaniments that mattered after one died were the good and noble deeds of one's life and an understanding of the Torah. Thus a Jew was buried in a plain shroud without pockets, for, "in the hour of man's departure from this world, neither gold, nor precious stones nor pearls accompany him but only Torah and good works."[3]

Even modern physics, amazingly, has provided a scientific framework for the possibility of life after death. For scientists whose understanding of the material world left no room for a supernatural realm or life beyond death, quantum physics has opened an entirely new dimension of thought by providing proof that the natural world does not actually obey the old laws of physics set forth by Isaac Newton. A physical particle, for example, can leave a space before it even arrives. Or it can be in two spaces at the same time (something all of us have probably wanted to do at some time in our lives). Dinesh D'Souza writes that the advent of modern physics, with its "complete reformulation of the laws of space, time and matter . . . has legitimated the possibility of the afterlife"[4]:

> The materialist objection has proved to be a dud; in fact, modern physics calls materialism itself into question. In a crucial area, and sometimes against the intentions of the scientists themselves, modern science has proven itself not the foe of religious believers, but an unexpected ally.[5]

So how do we know what to believe? Do we believe in heaven at all? Do we pick one of the many different religions' views? Do we stick with Isaac Newton and his version of the universe? Or do we dive into the great new world of quantum physics, where science and religion might unite once and for all?

Where Is the Answer?

Before we take such gargantuan leaps, we must ask ourselves if there is a single source that can answer our questions to ensure we do not fall into an eternal abyss.

There is. The Bible answers our questions so that we may live our lives free from the fear of losing our way and falling into a dark void at the end of our earthly existence. But if the Bible is, as I believe, the Word of God, we should begin our journey of discovery with "the people of the Book," the Jews. It is from the Jewish people that we have inherited the Bible that explains precisely what awaits us in heaven.

As a Jew myself, it breaks my heart to know that many of my people do not believe in heaven—or even in God. How can that be? How can many of the people especially chosen by God to share His love for us not believe in His Holy Scriptures?

We Jews have always been up for a good debate. We want to know the whys and hows of things. You will not find a single unquestionably authoritative teaching on the subject of the afterlife in the Talmud, Midrash or other texts, but rather a myriad of opposing viewpoints. When I was a boy, I, too, wanted an answer to the question of life after death. So I went to our rabbi, seeking his guidance. He was my spiritual leader, after all, so he should be the one I could count on to have the answers to my questions—but he did not. Instead, he told me that only God knows. I was crushed. I wanted assurance that there was a better life waiting beyond this one. Most of all, I wanted to know that my beloved grand-father, who had passed into eternity, was still alive and that I would see him again one day. But the rabbi could not give me that assurance.

I understand now that the Jewish people had been debating the existence of an afterlife for thousands of years. Let's take a minute to travel back to ancient Israel. At that time, Jewish thought was controlled by two powerful groups, the Pharisees and the Sadducees. They were similar to two competing political parties, but their influence was even more significant because they oversaw the hearts and souls of the Jewish people.

The Pharisees believed that the dead would be resurrected at the end of time. They taught that "souls have an immortal vigor in them" and that they would be either rewarded or punished "according as they have lived virtuously or viciously in this life."[6] The Sadducees were strict in their interpretations of the written Law. As they saw no clear teaching on the afterlife in the Torah, they rejected the idea completely. The Sadducees were mostly concerned with maintaining the rituals of the Temple and their place in those functions, and when the Second Temple was destroyed in AD 70, they disappeared from history.

Even though the Sadducees themselves vanished, their ideas did not entirely go with them. Many prominent Jews, past and present, likewise do not believe in an afterlife. Albert Einstein, for example, when asked if he believed in life after death, reportedly answered, "No, and one life is enough for me." Benedict de Spinoza, the great Jewish philosopher, believed that one's intellect returns to join with God but one's memories and attributes are lost forever. Which, I am sure, is not what most people want in an afterlife. They want to remember who they were in life so that they may be reunited with their loved ones.

But not all Jewish philosophers rejected the notion of an afterlife. Maimonides, the greatest Jewish philosopher of the medieval period, believed in "a revival of the dead at the time when it shall please the Creator."[7] I believe that anyone who reads his *Thirteen Principles of Faith* will be truly moved.

Indirect references to life after death may also be found in a number of references in the Pentateuch, the first five books of the Bible—such as in Genesis 25:8, where it states that after the death of Abraham, "he was gathered to his peoples." And in the apocryphal book of Jubilees, it is written, "And then the Lord will heal his servants, and they will rise up (from the dead) and see great peace" (Jubilees 23:30–31). Other old Jewish texts refer to *Olam Haba*, or the World to Come, describing man's soul returning to God upon death and the rising of all the dead at the end of time.

Who Will Go to Heaven?

The question remains: Who will be judged worthy to enter paradise? This question has also been debated over the centuries, with some Jewish leaders believing only the children of Israel will be granted entry, while others, like Rabbi Joshua ben Hananiah, said that "righteous Gentiles have a place in the world to come."[8] Maimonides agreed, saying, "The pious of all nations of the world have a portion in the world to come."[9]

Over the centuries, the resurrection of the dead became one of Judaism's essential tenets. For most Jews, there was no longer any doubt that the soul, man's quintessence and the spark of the divine within him, would live forever beyond the grave.

What can we know about heaven?

1. Heaven is a real place where the souls of the redeemed will live forever with God.
2. In heaven, there will be no sin, no sickness, no evil; just everlasting happiness. All pain suffered in this life

will be forgotten in the joy we experience in God's presence.

In the book of Revelation, heaven is depicted as a city constructed of the most precious stones and jewels of earth:

> The material of the city's wall was jasper, while the city was pure gold, clear as glass. The foundations of the city wall were decorated with every kind of precious stone—the first foundation was jasper; the second, sapphire; the third, chalcedony; the fourth, emerald; the fifth, sardonyx; the sixth, carnelian; the seventh, yellow topaz; the eighth, beryl; the ninth, topaz; the tenth, chrysoprase; the eleventh, jacinth; the twelfth, amethyst. And the twelve gates were twelve pearls—each of the gates was from a single pearl. And the street of the city was pure gold, transparent as glass. I saw no temple in her, for its Temple is ADONAI Elohei-Tzva'ot and the Lamb. And the city has no need for the sun or the moon to shine on it, for the glory of God lights it up, and its lamp is the Lamb.
>
> Revelation 21:18–23

Some scholars believe that this description of the apostle John is not to be taken literally. Instead, they say, he was using words his readers could understand to tell of something so wonderful that it is beyond description.

I am often asked what our bodies will be like in heaven. Will we look the same as we did here on earth? Will we be souls without bodies, more like spirits? If so, will we be visible to each other?

I look to the New Testament for some of the answers. Remember how Yeshua appeared to His disciples after He rose from the dead? He was not a ghost or spirit but a real body who could touch and be touched and eat, according to Luke 24:37–43. But He was also more than human. John 20:26 tells of Yeshua appearing among His followers even though the doors of their meeting room had been locked. Many, including John MacArthur, believe that our bodies will be like Yeshua's after He rose from the grave—glorified, able to partake of the pleasures of this life yet much more besides.[10] We will be free from sin and evil thoughts and desires, and this glory will give us a light, reflective of the brilliant splendor of the Messiah (see Revelation 1:16).

Only One Way to Heaven

Precious jewels and everlasting happiness aside, what is most important about heaven is that it is where we will be united with God the Creator and His Son, Yeshua.

It is only through Yeshua having sacrificed His life on the cross for us and our having accepted redemption through this sacrifice that we will be able to enter this eternal paradise.

Yeshua tells us, "I am the way, the truth, and the life! No one comes to the Father except through Me" (John 14:6). Nothing can be clearer than that. He also says,

> Do not let your heart be troubled. Trust in God; trust also in Me. In My Father's house there are many dwelling places. If it were not so, would I have told you that I am going to prepare a place for you? If I go and prepare a place for you, I will come again and take you to Myself, so that where I am you may also be.
>
> John 14:1–3

Focused on Heaven . . . and Earth

There is an old joke—forgive me if you have heard it—about a preacher who was getting his congregation fired up about the joys of heaven. When his sermon reached a fever pitch, he shouted, "If you want to go to heaven, stand up!"

Everybody stood up, except for one man in the next-to-last pew.

The preacher pounded on the pulpit and yelled, "I said, everybody who wants to go to heaven, stand up!"

The man did not budge.

The preacher glared at him and pointed. "What's the matter with you? Don't you want to go to heaven when you die?"

"When I *die?*" the man repeated. "Sure I do. I thought you were getting together a group to go right now."

This joke illustrates the truth of the old saying, "Everybody wants to go to heaven, but nobody wants to die."

The problem with that is that we are all going to die, someday. So we need to start planning right now where we will go when it happens. I know heaven is real and that the human mind cannot fully contemplate how wonderful it is going to be. I believe that when we get to heaven, we will all wonder why we were so afraid of dying. The time is now to make your reservation, by accepting Yeshua as your Lord and Savior.

It is never too early to start thinking about heaven—Karl Marx's opinion to the contrary. As you may remember, he called religion "the opiate of the people" because he felt that a belief in heaven led to a passive acceptance of oppression here on earth. "I may be suffering now," in other words, "but that's okay—pie in the sky will be mine bye and bye."

History shows that Marx got it wrong. Jews and Christians have led the fight against all sorts of evil, including Communism, Nazism and racism. Just look at the role Jews and Christian leaders played in America's civil rights movement. Today thousands of believers are on the front lines to uphold biblical values in our society. Thousands more are on the ground and working tirelessly in the world's poorest and most dangerous places, feeding the hungry, tending to the sick, providing shelter for the homeless—often putting their own lives at risk to serve others.

There is no truth at all to the saying that some people are too heavenly minded to be any earthly good.

As C. S. Lewis wrote,

> If you read history you will find that the Christians who did most for the present world were precisely those who thought most of the next. It is since Christians have largely ceased to think of the other world that they have become so ineffective in this.[11]

What about Hell?

John 3:36 tells us, "He who trusts in the Son has eternal life. He who does not obey the Son will not see life, but the wrath of God remains on him." What form will "God's wrath" take? Most cultures throughout history have believed in a place of punishment after death for those who have been corrupt or evil in this life. Although there have been many names for this "place," I am sure most of us would call it worthy of the name hell.

In ancient Egypt, it was believed that, after a person's death, he or she had to face a 42-judge tribunal who determined if the deceased had lived a righteous life. If so, they were welcomed into paradise; if not, they were cast out to a "devourer" to be tortured and annihilated. In Middle Eastern cultures, we see depictions of the netherworld (usually a miserable place below the earth) where souls not fit for paradise were relegated to suffer unbearable torments. From Europe and the Middle East to Africa to the Americas, cultures across the globe have had their own versions of this place of punishment. It seems we humans have been trying to understand what part hell plays in the afterlife from the beginning of man's time on earth.

What about Near-Death Experiences?

In recent times researchers have gathered dozens of accounts from people who have come back to life after being declared clinically dead. I interviewed a number of such people for my television show, *Jewish Voice with Jonathan Bernis*, and for my recent book *A Rabbi Looks at the Afterlife*, and they are all convinced of the reality of the afterlife.

Physicist Gerald Schroeder, whom I have quoted numerous times throughout this book, is a Jew who lives and works in Jerusalem. He writes that deaths recorded in the Torah followed a predictable pattern: Following death, the deceased was gathered to his people, and then his body was buried— sometimes months after the death and gathering. Schroeder believes that, based on various passages in the Torah (see Genesis 49–50), "the gathering is related to death and not to the physical act of burial in a family sarcophagus."[12] I agree completely with his assessment. Schroeder also sees parallels between the Torah's account of what happens at death and the stories told by people who have had near-death experiences: Being gathered to one's people "is exactly the experience that persons who have survived clinical death report. Deceased relatives reach out in vain to greet them as they return to the land of the living."[13]

Schroeder, as a scientist, feels compelled to conclude that some near-death experiences may be attributed to dreams brought on by chemical stresses in the brain during the dying process. But having interviewed many people who have returned from the brink of death, I am convinced that this is not the case. The experiences are too real, too vivid, and they cause lasting change in people's lives. They are not dreams or hallucinations. Every person I have interviewed insists that what they experienced was real. They saw and in some cases spoke to relatives who died years before. Some reported seeing people in heaven that they never expected to see there. All came back to this life with a stronger, deeper love for people. And those who say they went to heaven are no longer afraid of death. Some who went to a place of torment have changed their lives to ensure that they do not go back again the next time.

Here are some of the amazing stories I heard:

Dean Braxton: "When I left my body I also left the hospital, the earth and even this universe. I entered a very dark place with no light at all, and what I saw in the distance was heaven getting closer. . . . Nothing compared to the light I saw coming from heaven as I moved closer toward it. . . . When I arrived in heaven, all the members of my family who had come before me were there to greet me. Even though there were countless generations, I knew who each one was. The reason is the same as when Jesus was on the Mount of Transfiguration and Moses and Elijah wcrc with him. Although the apostles had never seen them before, they knew who they were. It's that kind of special knowledge that you rcccivc in heaven. When my relatives greeted me, I recognized some of them, but others had lived and died long before me. Yet we needed no introduction. It was generation after generation of those in my family who had accepted Jesus [Messiah] as Lord and Savior who were there to greet me. In heaven we have the opportunity to be that family we always wanted to be."[14]

Don Piper: "I was killed instantly in a terrible car crash. When you're dead an hour and a half, you're not nearly dead. You're totally dead. Four paramedics pronounced me dead at the scene of the accident. I'm only here because people prayed and God said yes. . . . All of them (the paramedics) were working on me, trying to bring me back and resuscitate me, trying to restore my life. But I was absent from the body and present with the Lord. . . . It was instantaneous. One second I was taking my last breath on the bridge, and the next I was standing outside one of the twelve gates of heaven. I was actually having a homecoming, a reunion with my loved ones, and when I saw their faces I knew where I was because I knew where they were. . . . My most vivid memory, and I wouldn't have thought this to be the case, was the music that surrounded me and invaded me. There were so many songs that were glorifying God, thousands of them really, that were rendered at the same time without chaos because they all fit and interfaced with each other. . . . I can close my eyes and still hear it as if I was there right now."[15]

Dr. Gary Wood: "Dying was the most peaceful and tranquil experience I ever had in my life. The first thing that happened was that I came straight out of my body. I was caught up in a massive, swirling funnel-shaped cloud and bright, brilliant light. I saw my body lying over the steering wheel, but by that time, I was already caught up in heaven. It was the most serene experience I've ever had in my life: joyful, exuberant, happy. . . . I saw an area where there were little children gathered on the grass, rolling around playing with a lion like you would play with a fluffy kitten. I saw kinds of animals in heaven that I've never seen before. People ask me if they'll be reunited with their pets in heaven and I tell them that, if it's part of God's plan, then they surely will. . . . I discovered later that I had been commissioned to make heaven real to this generation. That's why I was returned to earth."[16]

Howard Storm: "I heard people's voices calling my name. I went to the doorway and looked down the hallway. There were people standing there, shadowy and gray, and they were saying, 'Howard, hurry, come with us. We can't wait any longer.' And I replied, 'I'm sick, I need a doctor. I need surgery.' And they were saying, 'We don't have time for this. We know all about you. We've been waiting a long time for you.' . . . It got darker and darker, and I became increasingly frightened just by being with them. I knew that this was not a good situation. . . . I knew that, wherever I was, I was not in Paris, I was not in the hospital and I wasn't going to surgery. At that point I understood something bad was happening. I finally told them I wasn't going with them any further. [They began] biting, scratching and tearing at me. I was sure that this was all just the introduction to more horrible things they were going to do with me. The pain that they inflicted was terrible. I was being torn apart, bitten and scratched to pieces. . . . I called out to Him [Yeshua] to save me. And He came to me then . . . He reached down and touched me and all my wounds disappeared and I was made whole. But more importantly, He filled me with a love that I can't possibly begin to describe. There are no words adequate to express His love for us and His love, specifically, for me in that moment."[17]

A Glimpse of Hell

Listening to Howard Storm's story gave me chills. It changed his life completely—he went from being an atheist college professor to pastor of a Christian church. He blesses God every day for giving him a second chance.

Now, personally, I would rather not believe in hell. But whether I believe it exists or whether you believe it exists does not really matter. Hell will not go away just because we do not like the idea of it. And there are just too many references to it in Scripture for us to ignore. My everlasting salvation and yours depend on our believing in Yeshua and accepting the sacrifice He made on our behalf.

Some people question how a loving God, our Creator and Father, could even create such a terrible place. But theologian D. A. Carson says, "Hell is not a place where people are consigned . . . just [because they] didn't believe the right stuff. . . . [Hell is] filled with people who . . . want to be the center of the universe and who persist in their God-defying rebellion."[18]

Other theologians believe that if God did not create such a place of punishment for evil and defiant individuals, heaven would become meaningless.

For those who believe in a loving God and Creator but still doubt the existence of hell, I suggest a reading of the book of Matthew, in which twelve different passages relate to hell's existence. Matthew 13:49–50 says, "So it will be at the end of the age. The angels will come forth and separate the wicked from among the righteous and throw them into the fiery furnace; in that place will be weeping and gnashing of teeth."

Whether we like it or not, hell is something we dare not ignore.

A Jewish View of Hell

We Jewish people like to joke that if you have three Jews in a room, you end up with four opinions. And so it was with the ancient Jewish people and their views of hell. Though very few doubted its existence, there were many different ideas of what hell was, where it was and what happened to a person after they passed from this life.

For example, the Greek word *Hades* was used to describe a place where the dead wandered in damp, shadowy caves, weeping over the loss of their previous lives. That actually sounds pretty hellish to me, but it was not considered punishment to the ancient rabbis, just a place where the ghosts of the departed wandered for eternity.

Another word used in the Torah that gets confused with hell is *Sheol*. It has been translated several different ways, the most common being "grave." But it was never really considered to be a place of punishment, either, but rather a dwelling place for the dead.

The ancient term that most closely resembles our present-day vision of hell is *Gehenna*. It was an actual valley just south of the Old City of Jerusalem that had been used by the ancient Canaanites as a place of sacrifice to their god Molek. Because they practiced human sacrifice, the Jews later destroyed the grisly altars, and the surrounding valley became first a burial ground for criminals and later an enormous garbage dump. The prophet Jeremiah called the area the "Valley of Slaughter" (Jeremiah 19:6).

As the years passed, Gehenna became the Jewish term most closely resembling hell. One teaching in the Talmud states that souls sent to Gehenna first suffer with unrelenting itching, then burning fire and finally unbearable freezing cold.[19]

As Simcha Paull Raphael states,

The idea of a world of postmortem punishment was very real to the Rabbis and their disciples. They saw Gehenna as an abode of punishment for the person who did not live a righteous life in accordance with the ways of God and the Torah (Exodus Rabbah 2:2). That belief was central to their daily lives.[20]

Where the ancient rabbis had conflicting views about hell, Yeshua left no room for doubt. Hell is real. Hell is unmitigated torture. And hell is definitely a place no one wants to visit.

Now, it is true that many Christian churches do not teach that hell is a place of eternal torment—Seventh-day Adventists are one example. In 1995, the Church of England released an official document stating, in essence, that a loving God would not bring millions of souls into the world just to damn them to hell. And in a 1999 General Audience at the Vatican, Pope John Paul II said, "Hell is not a punishment imposed externally by God, but the condition resulting from attitudes and actions which people adopt in this life. . . . So eternal judgment is not God's work but is actually our own doing."

But many early Christian leaders had unwavering belief in a very different idea as to the nature of hell. The writings of Theophilus of Antioch in AD 181, Justin Martyr (*First Apology* 12) in AD 151 and Hippolytus in AD 212—to name a few—all cry out about the unending, excruciating torments awaiting the sinner who does not believe in and follow the precepts of God and His Redeemer, Jesus the Messiah.

Howard Storm says,

> Everything good comes from God. Life without God is when every good thing does not exist. There is no love, no light, no hope, no joy, no compassion, no truth, and no peace without God. . . . Even though God does not want one person to go to hell, God will not stop a person who is determined to go there. Whether we go to heaven or hell is determined by the choice we make. Do we accept God or not? If a person doesn't know the answer to that question, he has rejected God.[21]

Given the testimony of hell in the Bible, in ancient Jewish thought, among the early Church leaders, and from people like Howard who have glimpsed it firsthand, why do some Christian theologians and denominations still doubt the existence of a real and everlasting hell? Suffice it to say that it is simply a difficult concept to grasp. But I believe when our days on earth are over and we stand before our loving Father, if we have lived according to His Word, His infinite wisdom will be made known to us and our minds and hearts will at last be put at rest. "For now we see only a reflection as in a mirror; then we shall see face to face. Now I know in part;

then I shall know fully, even as I am fully known" (1 Corinthians 13:12 NIV).

Until that time, I will continue to stress what I truly believe. Hell is real and everlasting. It is a place of endless destruction (2 Thessalonians 1:9). It is a place where the fire never goes out (Mark 9:43). It is a place of weeping and gnashing of teeth (Matthew 25:30), of torment (Luke 16:23) where one can find no rest (Revelation 14:11).

Yeshua could not have made it clearer. And I believe without hesitation that I would give up everything in this earthly life to spend an eternity with my God and Savior and avoid the everlasting horrors of hell.

10

The Search for Meaning

And then quantum physics came onto the scene,
with its micro, micro world, only to prove that
there is no reality. Not even the one part in a million billion that seemed to be solid.

Gerald L. Schroeder[1]

Do you remember the movie *The Matrix*? It was a
fascinating film—the kind that gets people talking
and debating. Some have called it one of the best science
fiction movies ever.

To be honest, I do not remember much about the plot.
But I do remember the overall concept: Intelligent machines
had taken control of reality. The reality that human beings
thought they saw, heard, tasted and felt was actually nothing
more than a digital computer code—a matrix—developed
by those machines, which actually controlled humankind.

The Matrix pays homage to Plato's "Allegory of the Cave," which most of us have studied in school at one time or another. You may remember that Plato, speaking through the voice of Socrates, describes people who have spent their entire lives chained in a cave, facing a blank wall.

On the wall, they are able to see flickering shadows cast by things passing by a fire outside the cave. These shadows are as close as the cave dwellers ever get to reality. In fact, to those facing the wall, they *are* reality. Socrates goes on to say that most of us see the world in the same way. Only the wisest of men, the philosopher in this case, can understand that reality is far more than the shadows that pass on the wall before us.

Then quantum physics comes along, and we learn that much of what we have always considered to be solid matter is really nothing more than energy. (I should not say "nothing more," because energy is quite important. There is nothing inferior about it.) But until the last few decades, we thought that "matter" and "energy" were completely different things. Apparently, they are not.

Science has shown us that atoms consist almost entirely of empty space—even atoms that make up a heavy piece of steel. The electrons, protons and neutrons in an atom are infinitesimal and far apart. So the steel bar that seems solid and heavy really consists almost entirely of nothing!

As Gerald Schroeder puts it,

> Fighting all the way, we are being dragged, kicking and screaming, into accepting the truth that our material existence is more fiction than fact. . . . Physics has touched the metaphysical realm within which our physical illusion of reality is embedded. In crossing the threshold from the

physical to the metaphysical, science . . . has discovered the presence of the spiritual, for that is really what the metaphysical is within the land of the living.[2]

How Should We Then Live?

Yeshua had quite a bit to say about the foolishness of trading the joys of the world to come for the temporary pleasures of this one. In Mark 8:36, for example, he said that it does no good for a man to gain the whole world if he loses his soul in the process. There are many other verses throughout the New Testament that warn us not to become too attached to this world, or to put our hopes in this world. The apostle John writes, "Do not love the world or the things in the world. If anyone loves the world, the love of the Father is not in him" (1 John 2:15). Peter says, "For if—after escaping the world's pollutions through the knowledge of our Lord and Savior, Yeshua the Messiah—they again become entangled in these things and are overcome, the end for them has become worse than the beginning" (2 Peter 2:20). And Paul tells us that "this world in its present form is passing away" (1 Corinthians 7:31 NIV).

If our hope is in this world and this world alone, then we are standing on shaky ground. Yet this is exactly what thousands of people are doing—pursuing money, success, power, fame, adulation and other treasures of this world. In doing so they are chasing after sand. How foolish it is to invest all of our time and energy into building wealth in this world, like the farmer in Yeshua's parable:

The land of a certain rich man produced good crops. And he began thinking to himself, saying, "What shall I do? I

173

don't have a place to store my harvest!" And he said, "Here's what I'll do! I'll tear down my barns and build larger ones, and there I'll store all my grain and my goods. And I'll say to myself, 'O my soul, you have plenty of goods saved up for many years! So take it easy! Eat, drink, and be merry.'" But God said to him, "You fool! Tonight your soul is being demanded back from you! And what you have prepared, whose will that be?"

Luke 12:16–20

I believe there is a supernatural world, and that it is better and more real than the one we live in today. This is the world we should be investing in and planning for.

I mentioned earlier that I have had the privilege of interviewing quite a few people who suffered clinical death but came back to life, holding vivid memories from their near-death experiences. Many of them said that what they experienced in heaven made this world seem dreary and drab. Colors were brighter in heaven, music was more glorious, the grass, trees and flowers seemed more vibrantly alive— everything there seemed to appeal to the senses in a new and wonderful way.

Howard Storm is one who says he has come back from heaven. I told you a little bit of his story in the last chapter. Once, he was among those who ran after the pleasures of this life. Then his self-centered lifestyle took him to the edge of hell. That was where he called out to Jesus, and the Lord rescued him.

In his book *My Descent into Death*, Storm writes about many of the things he learned while on the other side of death. One of the most important is that God wants us to be His people and desires to spend time with us. "We think that this life in the world is important. It is only important as preparation for our eternal life. The only importance of this life is the choice we make to love God or not."[3]

Yeshua said something very similar, speaking through the apostle John: "I know your deeds, that you are neither cold nor hot. Oh, that you were either cold or hot! So because you are lukewarm, and neither cold nor hot, I am about to spew you out of My mouth" (Revelation 3:15–16).

Storm goes on to say, "The opposite of love is indifference. . . . To reject God so completely as to be indifferent is the most opposed to God we can be."[4]

I believe that Howard Storm may be right. And, like him, I am determined to live my life for God. It is only in a relationship with Him that we find the true meaning of life, as well as personal satisfaction and happiness.

I urge you to keep your eyes on God. Keep your eyes on the prize. As Paul wrote,

> Brothers and sisters, I do not consider myself as having taken hold of this. But this one thing I do: forgetting what is behind and straining toward what is ahead, I press on toward the goal for the reward of the upward calling of God in Messiah Yeshua.
>
> Philippians 3:13–14

Chasing after the Wind

In the first of the Ten Commandments, God tells us, "You shall have no other gods before Me" (Exodus 20:3). Yeshua told us to "seek first the kingdom of God and His righteousness" (Matthew 6:33).

175

Despite these Scriptures, people all around us are chasing after trifles like money, success, fame, adulation and even comfort.

A few weeks ago, one of the television networks ran a mini-series on Bernie Madoff, the former financial adviser who will spend the rest of his life in prison for defrauding hundreds of his clients out of billions of dollars. That is right—billions, with a *b*.

Madoff, as you may remember, was one of the most successful investors on Wall Street. Even when the economy took a major downturn and others were losing money hand over fist, Madoff's clients were prospering. It seemed too good to be true—and it was. In December 2008, Madoff admitted that the wealth management of his company was nothing more than an elaborate Ponzi scheme. In case you are not familiar with the term, a Ponzi scheme is one in which earlier investors are paid off with money raised from newer investors, instead of with money earned through investments. In other words, no real profit is made. When the pool of new investors dries up, so does the income.

On March 12, 2009, Madoff admitted to operating the largest private Ponzi scheme in history. He was sentenced to 150 years in prison and ordered to pay restitution of $170 billion. According to authorities, Madoff had pulled off the largest accounting fraud in American history.

What caused Bernie Madoff to swing so far off the tracks? He knew how to run an investment firm that stayed within the boundaries of the law. He could have been quite successful at it. But he was not content to do that because the profits were not big enough and the competition was too tough. He was obsessed with making money, and he destroyed many lives in his pursuit for riches—including that of his son, Mark, who hanged himself on the second anniversary of his father's arrest. Bernie Madoff's brother, Peter, was sentenced to ten years in prison. And hundreds, perhaps thousands, of people were wiped out financially. All because money was Bernie Madoff's idol.

And that makes me think of Elvis Presley.

You may be thinking, "What in the world does Elvis Presley have to do with Bernie Madoff?" Elvis Presley had it all, and he gained it honestly. He sold hundreds of millions of records. He starred in dozens of movies. He performed to adoring crowds all over the world, lived in a house as big as a palace and enjoyed every type of pleasure this life has to offer.

All that is true. But Elvis Presley also died of a drug overdose at the age of 42—and, due to his drug abuse, spent the last several months of his life as what amounted to a burned-out caricature of himself.

What makes the story even more tragic is that Elvis Presley grew up singing in church. He was baptized when he was nine years old and felt called to become a pastor. But when a new kind of music called rock 'n' roll came along and chose Elvis as its king, he spent the rest of his life chasing fame and fortune. I believe he also spent the rest of his life torn between two worlds. He felt a strong pull to God and godly things; you can tell that from all the albums of gospel music he recorded. But at the same time he wanted to live up to his image as the king of rock 'n' roll. He wanted to be cool, to live on the edge and try everything this world had to offer. Like Bernie Madoff, he was focused on the wrong things.

Just imagine if Elvis had given all of his energy, talent and charisma to lifting up the name of Jesus. I believe he could have done great things for the Kingdom of God. That is to say, even though Elvis Presley is considered to be one of the greatest figures of the twentieth century, I believe he settled for much less than he could have been—when you look through the eyes of eternity.

One more: The other day I saw a short news story hailing the fact that a 25th-anniversary edition of Nirvana's first album, *Nevermind*, is about to be released. If you were around in the early 1990s, and if you are a fan of contemporary music, you certainly remember Nirvana, the originators of "grunge" rock. After Nirvana appeared on the scene, the city of Seattle briefly became the capital of rock 'n' roll. The members of Nirvana wore plaid, so teenagers all over the world were suddenly wearing the same.

Kurt Cobain, the lead singer, guitarist and songwriter of Nirvana, was hailed as a musical genius. But on April 5, 1994, just three years after Nirvana hit it big, Kurt Cobain took his own life. He was only 27 years old. He thus joined a long line of talented people who died at the apex of their careers. People like Janis Joplin, Jimi Hendrix, Jim Morrison, Marilyn Monroe, Philip Seymour Hoffman, John Belushi, Chris Farley, Cory Monteith, Whitney Houston, Michael Jackson, Amy Winehouse . . . the list goes on and on.

I am not judging Kurt Cobain. I do not really know anything about him—except that if he had given his life to the Lord and served Him, he would not have died at the age of 27.

Too many people are giving up God's best for them to chase after the wind. James 4:14 tells us, "What is your life?

For you are a vapor that appears for a little while and then vanishes."

Given the uncertainty and temporary nature of human life, it seems that the wisest thing we can possibly do is keep our eyes on eternity. This world is not the only world, this life is not the only life. For those who trust in God, the best is yet to come.

Remember Who You Are

What is the meaning of life?

As Ecclesiastes says, "Now all has been heard; here is the conclusion of the matter: Fear God and keep his commandments, for this is the duty of all mankind" (Ecclesiastes 12:13 NIV).

Yeshua told us how we are to serve God: "You shall love ADONAI your God with all your heart, and with all your soul, and with all your strength, and with all your mind; and your neighbor as yourself" (Luke 10:27).

You are not an accident. You are not a random combination of chemicals. You are a living, breathing soul, a special creation of a loving God. This life is your preparation for the life to come. It is like a short introduction to a novel with hundreds or even thousands of pages—but, oh, what a difference a great introduction can make. I like the way Howard Storm puts it:

> In heaven we will look back upon our lives with the same amusement that we feel when we look at our childhood hopes and fears. Why didn't I say, "Yes," to God sooner? Why did I wait so long? . . .
>
> Jesus is the way, the truth, and the life. He is the best friend you will ever have.[5]

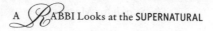

Have you surrendered your life to the One who gave His for you?

If not, please do it now. Take a step outside the confines of this physical world into a limitless supernatural existence that will last forever. Make a decision you will never, ever regret—even for all eternity.

Notes

Chapter 1: Dust in the Wind?

1. Gerald L. Schroeder, *The Hidden Face of God* (New York: Free Press, 2001), 1.

Chapter 2: Not Quite, Mr. Darwin

1. Francis S. Collins, *The Language of God* (New York: Free Press, 2006), 97.
2. Charles Darwin, *On the Origin of Species* (New York: Penguin, 1958), 452.
3. Ibid., 457.
4. Antony Flew, *There Is a God* (New York: HarperCollins, 2007), 75–76.
5. Ibid., 76–77.
6. Max Jammer, *Einstein and Religion* (Princeton, N.J.: Princeton University Press, 1999), 48.
7. Albert Einstein, *The Quotable Einstein*, ed. Alice Calaprice (Princeton, N.J.: Princeton University Press, 2005), 195–96.
8. Collins, *Language of God*, 107.
9. John Polkinghorne, *Belief in God in an Age of Science* (New Haven, Conn.: Yale University Press, 2003), 10.
10. Flew, *There Is a God*, 163.
11. Charles Darwin, *The Autobiography of Charles Darwin, 1809–82* (New York: Harcourt & Brace, 1958), 93.
12. Schroeder, *Hidden Face of God*, 61–62.
13. Collins, *Language of God*, 90–91.
14. Schroeder, *Hidden Face of God*, 46.
15. Jeremy Rifkin, *Algeny: A New Word—A New World* (New York: Penguin, 1984), 168.
16. Freeman Dyson, "Progress in Religion" (acceptance speech for the Templeton Prize for Progress in Religion, Washington, D.C., May 16, 2000), https://www.edge.org/conversation/freeman_dyson-progress-in-religion.

17. Stephen Hawking, *A Brief History of Time* (New York: Bantam, 1998), 144.

18. Collins, *Language of God*, 76.

19. Hugh Ross, *The Creator and the Cosmos* (Glendora, Calif.: Reasons to Believe, 2001), 211.

20. Philip Yancey, *Soul Survivor* (Colorado Springs, Colo.: WaterBrook, 2001), 3.

21. Hugh Ross, "Fine Structure Constant," Reasons to Believe, February 1, 2004, http://www.reasons.org/articles/fine-structure-constant.

22. Hugh Ross, "Designer Water," Reasons to Believe, March 2, 2005, http://www.reasons.org/articles/designer-water.

23. Hugh Ross, "Planetary System Stability," Reasons to Believe, March 1, 2004, http://www.reasons.org/articles/planetary-system-stability.

24. Hugh Ross, "Solar Luminosity Stability," Reasons to Believe, November 16, 2004, http://www.reasons.org/articles/solar-luminosity-stability.

25. David Briggs, "Science, Religion are Discovering Commonality in Big Bang Theory," *Los Angeles Times*, May 2, 1992, http://articles.latimes.com/1992-05-02/local/me-1350_1_big-bang-theory.

26. Eric Metaxas, "Science Increasingly Makes the Case for God," *The Wall Street Journal*, December 25, 2014.

27. Fred Hoyle, "The Big Bang in Astronomy," *New Scientist* 92, no. 1280 (1981): 527.

28. Fred Hoyle, "Evolution from Space" (Omni lecture, Royal Institution, London, U.K., January 12, 1982).

29. Flew, *There Is a God*, 131.

30. George Wald, "Life and Mind in the Universe," *International Journal of Quantum Chemistry* 26, supplement no. 11 (1984): 1–15. doi:10.1002/qua.560260703.

31. Flew, *There Is a God*, 183.

32. Ibid., 182–83.

Chapter 3: The Invisible World

1. Ben Alexander, *Out from Darkness* (Joplin, Mo.: ESP Ministries, 1988), 28–29.

2. Michael Lipka, "18 Percent of Americans Say They've Seen a Ghost," Pew Research Center, October 30, 2015, http://www.pewresearch.org/fact-tank/2015/10/30/18-of-americans-say-theyve-seen-a-ghost/.

3. "Are UFOs Real? Famous People Who Believed," *Daily Telegraph*, April 22, 2009, http://www.telegraph.co.uk/technology/5201410/Are-UFOs-real-Famous-people-who-believed.html.

4. Bill Myers and Dave Wimbish, *The Dark Side of the Supernatural* (Grand Rapids, Mich.: Zondervan, 1999), 12–14.

5. Ruth Montgomery, *Aliens among Us* (New York: Putnam and Sons, 1985), 44.

6. Kendall, "Angel at the Accident," October 2006, http://paranormal.about.com/library/blstory_october06_12.htm.

7. Many of the details of this story are found in Lynn Picknett, *Flights of Fancy* (New York: Ballentine, 1987), 173–76.

8. C. S. Lewis, *The Screwtape Letters* (New York: MacMillan, 1959), 3.

Chapter 4: Ghosts and the Bible

1. Myers and Wimbish, *Dark Side*, 108.
2. Jenny Randles and Peter Hough, *The Afterlife* (New York: Berkley Books, 1993), 114–15.
3. Alexander, *Out from Darkness*, 37.
4. Ibid., 108.
5. Jack Deere, *Surprised by the Power of the Spirit* (Grand Rapids, Mich.: Zondervan, 1993), 214–15.
6. Brad Steiger, *The UFO Abductors* (New York: Berkeley Books, 1988), 30–32.

Chapter 5: Sin and Righteousness

1. Arthur Kac, *The Messiahship of Jesus* (Chicago: Moody, 1980), 207.
2. Clay H. Trumbull, *The Blood Covenant* (Kirkwood, Mo.: Impact Books, 2009); quote within blurb is unattributed.
3. Ibid., 4–5.
4. Ibid., 62.
5. Ibid., 53.
6. Ibid., 5–6.
7. Ibid., 38.
8. Ibid., 273.
9. Ibid., 281–82.
10. Jonathan Bernis, *A Rabbi Looks at Jesus of Nazareth* (Minneapolis: Chosen, 2011), 189–90.
11. Lee Strobel, *The Case for Christ* (Grand Rapids, Mich.: Zondervan, 1998), 298–300.
12. Alexander Roberts and James Donaldson, eds., *The Writings of Justin Martyr and Athenagoras* (Edinburgh, Scotland: Murray and Gibb, 1868), 235.
13. John Stott, *Basic Christianity* (Downers Grove, Ill.: InterVarsity, 2008), 62.
14. Ibid., 307.
15. Lee Strobel, *The Case for Easter* (Grand Rapids, Mich.: Zondervan, 1998), 21.
16. Ibid.
17. Ibid., 25.
18. Bert Thompson and Brad Harrub, "An Examination of the Medical Evidence for the Physical Death of Christ," *Reason and Revelation* 22, no. 1 (2002), http://www.apologeticspress.org/apPubPage.aspx?pub=1&issue=525&article=130.
19. Josh McDowell, *Evidence That Demands a Verdict* (San Bernardino, Calif.: Campus Crusade for Christ, 1972), 208.

Chapter 6: The Problem of Evil

1. Harold S. Kushner, *When Bad Things Happen to Good People* (New York: Random House, 1981), 180.
2. Flew, *There Is a God*, 42.
3. Ibid.
4. C. S. Lewis, *The Problem of Pain* (New York: MacMillan, 1973), 69, 33.

5. John R. W. Stott, *The Cross of Christ* (Downers Grove, Ill.: InterVarsity Press, 1986), 335–36.

6. Avoda Zara 17a.

7. Lewis, *Problem of Pain*, 15.

8. Philip Yancey, *I Was Just Wondering* (Grand Rapids, Mich.: Eerdmans, 1998), 33.

9. Weisenthal's story is told in Yancey, *Just Wondering*, 71–75.

10. Corrie ten Boom, *Tramp for the Lord* (Grand Rapids, Mich.: Revell, 2000), 82.

Chapter 7: In Sickness and in Health

1. C. S. Lewis, *The Joyful Christian* (New York: MacMillan, 1996), 97.

2. John Wimber, *Power Healing* (San Francisco: Harper & Row, 1987), 50–51.

3. Carol Wimber, "How the Vineyard Began," Vineyard Churches U.K. and Ireland, August 15, 2012, http://www.vineyardchurches.org.uk/resources/articles /how-the-vineyard-began/.

4. Wimber, *Power Healing*, 52.

5. Ibid., 32.

6. Ibid., 54.

7. Deere, *Surprised*, 154.

8. Robby Dawkins, *Do What Jesus Did* (Minneapolis: Chosen, 2013), 125–26.

9. Dawkins, *Identity Thief*, 92.

10. Toby Druin, "While Teaching on Psalm 103, Former Pastor's Voice Is Healed," *The Baptist Press*, January 29, 1993, 24.

11. Wimber, *Power Healing*, 22.

Chapter 8: Miracles or Meshugas?

1. C. S. Lewis, *Miracles* (New York: Simon & Schuster, 1996), 10–11.

2. Ibid., 13.

3. Ibid., 130–31.

4. Deere, *Surprised*, 28–29.

5. Deere, *Surprised*, 156.

6. Erich Bridges, "Miracles on the Border: Syrians Encounter Jesus," *Baptist Press*, November 16, 2012, www.bpnews.net/39178/miracles-on-the-border -Syrians-encunter-Jesus.

7. Micael Grenholm, "Miracles in the Middle East," *Holy Spirit Activism*, Holyspiritactivism.com/miracles-in-the-middle-east.

8. David Rupert, "Miracles in the Middle East: Is There Hope in the Chaos?" *Patheos*, October 5, 2015, www.patheos.com/blogs/davidrupert/miracles-in-the -middle-east-is-there-hope-in-the-chaos.

9. Don Richardson, *Eternity in Their Hearts* (Ventura, Calif.: Regal, 1984), 102.

Chapter 9: More Than Fairy Tales

1. Howard Storm, *My Descent into Death* (New York: Doubleday, 2005), 117.

2. See, for example, Albert L. Winseman, "Eternal Destinations: Americans Believe in Heaven, Hell," Gallup, May 25, 2004, http://www.gallup.com/poll/11770

/eternal-destinations-americans-believe-heaven-hell.aspx and Caryle Murphy, "Most Americans Believe in Heaven . . . and Hell," Pew Research Center, November 10, 2015, http://www.pewresearch.org/fact-tank/2015/11/10/most-americans -believe-in-heaven-and-hell/.

3. Pirke Avot 6:9.

4. Dinesh D'Souza, *Life After Death: The Evidence* (Washington, D.C.: Regnery, 2009), 74.

5. Ibid., 89.

6. Flavius Josephus, *Antiquities* 18.1.3.

7. United Noahide Academies, "Foundations of Torah, Principles of Faith, and Moshiach (the Messiah)," 2011, http://asknoah.org/wp-content/uploads/UNA -Class2-Lesson1.pdf.

8. Tosefta Sanhedrin 13:2.

9. Mishneh Torah Repentance 3:5.

10. See John F. MacArthur, *The Glory of Heaven* (Wheaton, Ill.: Crossway, 1996), 125, 134.

11. Wayne Martindale, *Beyond the Shadow Lands* (Wheaton, Ill.: Crossway, 2005), 47.

12. Schroeder, *Hidden Face of God*, 171.

13. Ibid., 171–172.

14. Dean Braxton, interview by Jonathan Bernis, *Jewish Voice with Jonathan Bernis*, November 3–9, 2014.

15. Don Piper, interview by Jonathan Bernis, *Jewish Voice with Jonathan Bernis*, unaired.

16. Gary Wood, interview by Jonathan Bernis, *Jewish Voice with Jonathan Bernis*, November 17–23, 2014.

17. Howard Storm, interview by Jonathan Bernis, *Jewish Voice with Jonathan Bernis*, November 10–16, 2014.

18. Lee Strobel, *The Case for Faith* (Grand Rapids, Mich.: Zondervan, 2000), 175.

19. p San Hedrin 29b.

20. Simcha Paull Raphael, *Jewish Views of the Afterlife* (Lanham, Md.: Rowman and Littlefield, 2009), 142.

21. Storm, *Descent*, 52–54.

Chapter 10: The Search for Meaning

1. Schroeder, *Hidden Face of God*, 4.

2. Ibid., 170.

3. Storm, *Descent*, 64–65.

4. Ibid., 65.

5. Ibid., 146.

Jonathan Bernis is the president and CEO of Jewish Voice Ministries International and the author of several books, including *A Rabbi Looks at Jesus of Nazareth*, *A Rabbi Looks at the Last Days*, *A Rabbi Looks at the Afterlife* and *A Hope and a Future*. A Jewish believer in Jesus, he has been in Messianic Jewish ministry for more than 35 years and is the host of *Jewish Voice with Jonathan Bernis*, a daily television program seen on Christian networks across the globe. Jonathan and his wife, Elisangela, are the parents of two daughters, Liel and Hannah, and reside in Phoenix, Arizona.

To learn more about Jonathan and Jewish Voice Ministries International, please call or write, or visit our website:

Jewish Voice Ministries International
P.O. Box 31998
Phoenix, AZ 85046-1998
Phone: (602) 971-8501
Fax: (602) 971-6486
Toll-free 24-hour order line: 1-800-306-0157
www.jewishvoice.org

More from
Jonathan Bernis

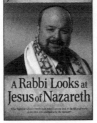

Raised in a traditional Jewish family, Jonathan Bernis was taught that "Jews don't—and can't!—believe in Jesus." Yet in his study of the Scriptures, including the Torah, Bernis found overwhelming evidence that Jesus of Nazareth really is the Jewish Messiah. Join Bernis on his journey of discovering Jesus, and equip yourself with the knowledge you need to gently share your faith with a Jewish friend.

A Rabbi Looks at Jesus of Nazareth

With a startling, hopeful perspective, Messianic Rabbi Jonathan Bernis reveals the most obvious signs that the last days are upon us—and they may not be what you think. Unpacking the mysteries of this cryptic time, he shows how biblical prophecies are being fulfilled right now in Israel. Discover how you can help usher in God's Kingdom!

A Rabbi Looks at the Last Days

✔Chosen